Utopian Literature

Utopian Literature

A Bibliography

with

A Supplementary Listing of
Works Influential in Utopian Thought

BY

G<small>LENN</small> N<small>EGLEY</small>

T<small>HE</small> R<small>EGENTS</small> P<small>RESS</small> <small>OF</small> K<small>ANSAS</small>
L<small>AWRENCE</small>

©Copyright 1977 by The Friends of Duke University Library
Printed in the United States of America

Library of Congress Cataloging in Publication Data
Negley, Glenn Robert, 1907-
Utopian literature.

Includes indexes.
1. Utopias—Bibliography—Union lists. I. Title.
Z7164.U8N43 [HX806] 016.321'07 77-8265
ISBN 0-7006-0164-3

To

Benjamin E. Powell

Librarian
Duke University
1946-1975
Friend of Utopia

Contents

Acknowledgments

It is questionable whether any other institution would have offered encouragement and support for a project which thirty years ago must have seemed somewhat bizarre—the assembly of a collection of utopian literature in the Rare Book Room of the library. My gratitude to the Duke University Library is, therefore, beyond expression; were I to name all the persons encompassed by that gratitude, a roster of the staff would have to be included. Practically, let the mention of a few serve as appreciation for the whole: Benjamin E. Powell, Librarian of the University during the period of this acquisition; Gertrude Merritt, Associate Librarian; John L. Sharpe III, Curator of Rare Books; Florence Blakely and Mary Canada of the Reference Department; and the most helpful assistants of all these people. My colleagues have been a source of information about obscure and forgotten works which no one person could have discovered, notably, at Duke University, John Alden and Clarence Gohdes; my most amiable collaborator on *The Quest for Utopia*, J. Max Patrick, was an inspiration and remains a scholarly guide; Kenneth M. Roemer has contributed to my knowledge of American utopian writing. Finally, a note of appreciation is due Stuart A. Teitler, bibliophile and bookman extraordinary, whose knowledge and acumen have contributed to the building of the collection.

Introduction

The purpose of this bibliography is to provide for scholars a listing of an important and neglected area of Western literature. The few reliable bibliographies of utopian thought are limited in either chronological or geographical coverage. It is hoped that this broader survey will be helpful to scholars in many fields who are interested in a particular time-span or linguistic area. A surprising number of utopian works, many of them by notable authors, seem to have been almost completely forgotten and an assessment of their influence thereby ignored—perhaps one of the most serious deficiencies of appraisal in social, political, cultural, and literary historical analysis.

The literature of Greece and Rome is well known and readily available; hence it is not included in this bibliography.[1] As for the hiatus from *ca.* 200 B.C. to 1500 A.D., it is my judgment that the following pronouncement is essentially correct: "The fact remains that from the time of the ancient Greeks till the revival of their influence in the Renaissance, the realms of Utopia, like the glories of Atlantis, disappeared from sight."[2] This bibliography begins, therefore, with the stirrings of utopian thought in the sixteenth century, encompasses the enthusiastic and fruitful revival of utopian speculation in the seventeenth century, and advances through the centuries to the present.

DEFINITION

Perhaps no other words in our language are more subject to random meaning than *utopia* and *utopian*. Common usage will undoubtedly continue to employ these terms in a pejorative manner to indicate the impracti-

---

[1] For a brief but adequate survey of this literature, see Glenn Negley and J. Max Patrick, "Classical Utopias 900 B.C.–200 B.C.," in *The Quest for Utopia* (New York, 1952), chap. 14.

[2] *Ibid.,* p. 258.

cal, the visionary, the fantastic, even the idiotic. On the other hand, the range of the literature is so wide that any attempt at a reasonably specific definition of what may properly be termed *utopia* is extremely difficult. Some such effort, however, is necessary, else any purported listing of utopian works would proliferate endlessly into pheripheries of almost all social, political, even religious, speculation.

This bibliography has used, as nearly as is possible, the definition of utopia advanced in *The Quest for Utopia*.[3] As defined there, a utopia is first a fictional work (thus distinguished from political tracts and dissertations); it describes a particular state or community, even though that may be as limited as a small group or so extensive as to encompass the world or the universe (thus a statement of principles or procedural reforms is not a utopia); its theme is the political structure of that fictional state or community (thus a mere Robinsonade, adventure narrative, or science fantasy does not qualify as utopian).

Admittedly, strict adherence to such definitive restrictions is very difficult, if not impossible; but some grounds are thereby provided for the elimination of a vast lot of writing which has often been indiscriminately labeled utopian. At the very least, it is an effort to establish some denotative and connotative sense for the term utopia.

Perhaps the most straightforward claim for the right of definition is acquaintance with the subject matter to justify the often difficult and delicate decision as to whether a particular work should properly be classified as a utopia. Even on that ambigious basis, no two persons, however knowledgeable in the field, could be expected to agree on all the items in such a bibliography. It will suffice for present purposes if some reasonable, even though less than exact, definitive exclusion has been operative.

It may be argued that such a definition is too formal, too stylistic, but how can a literary genre be distinguished except by its content and structure? A sonnet is a sonnet by definition, be its execution admirable or execrable. So a utopia is a utopia by definition, be its content profound or trivial, its structure a literary delight or a travesty of prose expression. The Declaration of Independence or the Communist Manifesto may be said to be an expres-

---

[3] *Ibid.,* pp. 4–5. Professor Darko Suvin of McGill University has commented on this definition: "Professors Negley and Patrick seem to have been the first expressly to enunciate a differentiation between the utopia of political scientists and *Geisteswissenschaftler* . . . and that of the literary critics and theorists. . . . Their pioneering status is evident in a certain uneasy compromise with the older conception which they are just abandoning." *Studies in the Literary Imagination* (Atlanta, Ga.), Fall 1973, pp. 130–31.

Introduction

sion of profound political and philosophical ideals, but neither is a utopia. As a sonnet may be maudlin, so a utopia may present a fantastic or even a silly example of ideals, but it is a utopia. The distinction of utopia as a form of literature is not arbitrary; a long history of usage and context, despite variations, justifies such definition, as descriptive limitations are justified in the classification of poetry, despite the manifold forms of its expression. Lexicographers have been remiss in their failure to recognize that there are substantial grounds for adducing a more precise definition of utopia than "imaginary," "fantastic," "impractical," "chimerical." It is extraordinary that an area of our literature distinguished by contributions from some of our most prestigious authors should have been so ill-treated, while that recently spawned bastard form of literary effusion called "science fiction" has received academic and critical attention, even though the majority of its practitioners are hack writers.

Dystopia is an ill-sounding word first coined, I believe, in *The Quest for Utopia* in 1952. While the word may sound like the nomenclature for some kind of disease, it would be quite unfair to regard dystopias as a kind of cancerous growth in the body of utopian literature. True, some dystopias are so pessimistic about man and his ideals that they attack the very existence and well-being of utopian idealization itself. The greater number of dystopias, however, are given to satire, to playful jesting at pomposities, and often to astute and acerbic reactions to utopian excesses. Since Aristophanes lampooned Plato in *The Ecclesiazusae,* dystopia has been a continuing form of social, political, and literary criticism. The accomplishment of effective satire and burlesque requires considerable literary skill; consequently, some of the nicest pieces of prose in the general field of utopian literature are to be found in the dystopias.

The division of listed works between the bibliography proper and the supplementary listing of influential works is at variance with usual bibliographical format. However subject to question, this classification has been adopted in keeping with the definition of utopian literature used as a premise here. The supplementary listing is considered an important and useful aid to research in utopian literature. Admittedly, the selection here is almost entirely arbitrary; what constitutes significance and influence in these fringe areas is almost completely an arguable matter. Justification can only be the purpose of suggesting research on the nature and sources of utopian writing. The intent is to provide some indication of possible influence on utopian thought in particular historical periods. The hope is that, as in fictional detection (to which this kind of research bears some resemblance), one clue may lead to others and thus to further analysis of the utopian speculation of an author or of a period. The short-title index and the chronological index include both listings to facilitate this association of authors and possible sources of influence on their thought. Very rarely indeed does the utopist in his work of fiction refer to writers or works which significantly shaped his thinking, but such influences there indisputably were; to explore these historical continuities of intellectual and philosophical development is a challenge.

HISTORICAL CONTINUITY

Generalizations about utopian literature are even more hazardous than most such simplifications. The content, the intent, and the expression are so varied and diverse in all historical periods that trends and continuity are indeed very difficult to establish. Anyone with even a limited knowledge of utopian writing can immediately produce exceptions to any generalized reduction. Acquaintance with some twelve hundred works which can be termed utopian or directly influential in utopian thought indicates, however, that it is possible to detect in this voluminous contribution certain marked changes of attention and interest, whatever exceptions may be adduced to the general pattern of thought influencing the overwhelming majority of utopists.

The sixteenth century presents a rather tentative groping about for the long-forsaken concept of man's utopia. The prevailing influence of religion prompted a number of works which might be called the Perfect Christian Prince genre, on the fringe of proper utopian construction, but influential and significant in respect to their audience, wide for that time. There was also a revival of interest in ancient civilizations and their structure; many were idealized almost to the extreme of fantasy (as in works by Contarini, Furió Ceriol, Guevara, and Paruta) to provide comparison with the inadequacies and inequities of their own day.

After this rather fumbling return to the utopian enterprise, the seventeenth century erupted with such vigor and enthusiasm for this novel subject of attention that it remains the most important period in the long history of utopia; men eagerly turned their attention from the City of God to the City of Man.

The seventeenth century produced noteworthy and memorable examples of all the forms which were to become characteristic of this kind of political expression: the progressive, regressive, totalitarian, republican, technological, fantastic, and dystopian. The influence of this outpouring of utopian ideas on the Western world is incalculable; certainly they were a major factor in stirring men and governments to the revolutionary changes of the late eighteenth and nineteenth centuries.

Introduction

The corporate organization of Campanella's *City of the Sun* could very well serve as a model for a current totalitarian society if the dictators were sufficiently subtle and capable of employing Campanella's insidious system of using the dread of a hierarchical and compulsory administration of confessionals, including public confession of sins against the state. In this manner, a self-perpetuating troika of dictators maintained absolute power—and order. Not even the traumatic predictions of Orwell's *1984* suggest a more absolute tyranny. Campanella was an apostle of the doctrine that the end justifies the means if the end appears essential to the preservation of the social structure; and to him the establishment of law and order seemed paramount in the Italy of his day.[4]

The most influential utopia of this fertile period was James Harrington's *Oceana,* surely one of the dullest, most pedantic, and pedestrian works in the literature. Yet the ideas and the ideals of this and other political works by Harrington were so eminently sensible and desirable that they commanded attention. It is only in retrospect that we appreciate how truly utopian some of Harrington's proposals were in the seventeenth century; it was more than a hundred years before the practical realization of these ideals began to be achieved in the revolutionary movements of the eighteenth century.

The promise of technological achievement was, of course, thoroughly explored by Bacon in *New Atlantis.* His anticipations were indeed astute, if not intuitive—including airships, submarines, the telephone, and even prediction of the laser beam. It is a great pity that his utopia should have remained "A Worke Unfinished" and that we cannot know his more considered judgment as to what kind of social and political structure would be appropriate to this technological world of the future, a critical concern of present day utopian contemplation.

Utopias with a religious orientation, somewhat regressive in nature, are best represented by Andreä's *Reipublicae Christianopolitanae Descriptio* and Samuel Gott's *Novae Solymae.* In a real sense these were efforts to effect a transition from the dominance of the religious establishment which had for so long prevailed to the complexities of society becoming evident even to the most pious observer.

Fantasy as a vehicle for utopian and dystopian thought finds delightful expression in Cyrano de Bergerac's somewhat whimsical explorations in *Histoire Comique des États et Empires de la Lune* and *L'Histoire des*

---

[4] The most comprehensive work in English on Campanella, with an excellent bibliography, is Bernardino M. Bonansea, *Tommaso Campanella: Renaissance Pioneer of Modern Thought* (Washington, D.C., 1969).

États et Empires du Soleil. Even more whimsical was the resolution of the problem of sex in utopia—by a monk, Gabriel de Foigny, in *Terra Australis Incognita.* In this society of hermaphrodite nudists, any child who happens to be born with either sex dominant is immediately strangled as a monster.

Dystopias too received due attention in this century of utopian effluence. The most widely known is that of Joseph Hall, *Mundus Alter et Idem,* which has been much reprinted and translated. Of greater interest and worth is the now almost forgotten dystopia of Traino Boccalini, *De' Ragguagli di Parnaso.* Boccalini may or may not have been influenced by the earlier work of Giordano Bruno, *Spaccio de la Bestia Trionfante;* at any rate, the two works employ the same format: a conference of the gods on the affairs of man. Boccalini suffered severely for his dystopian attack on papal power, the Spanish influence in Italy, and the Inquisition, for it is almost certain that he was assassinated by hirelings of one of those establishments which he had subjected to ridicule and invective.[5]

The wide-ranging, catholic, and adventurous spirit which animated the utopists of the seventeenth century changed so abruptly that it is difficult to account for the startling reversal of mood and intent. The institutions of society were the subject of attention during that period; to be sure, the writings were an attack on prevailing institutional structures, but they were, almost without exception, concerned with the creation and maintenance of more desirable and ideal institutional organizations. Perhaps it was disillusion and disgust with existing institutions and governments—an attitude undoubtedly encouraged by the seventeenth century utopists—that inclined men to an abrupt rejection of political organization and administration.

Whatever the manifold reasons, and they would be difficult to unravel, during the eighteenth century the general mood and interest of utopists turned to a celebration of arcadian simplicity and the beneficence of man in a state of nature. The philosophy is often called Rousseauistic, but its development began before Rousseau presented his garbled exposition of the theme. The major work of this transition is Fénelon's *Suite du Quatrième Livre de l'Odysée d'Homère (The Adventures of Telemachus).* This work is extraordinary not because of its content, but because of the attention it received and continues to receive (see note in bibliography); it is one of the few works other than the Bible which have been accorded the distinction of a six-language, polyglot edition. The reasons for this attention are very unclear, to say the least, for intrinsically Fénelon does not merit such acclaim.

---

[5] See Richard Thomas, "Trajano Boccalini's 'Ragguagli di Parnaso' and Its Influence upon English Literature," *Aberstwyth Studies,* vol. 3, 1922.

Introduction

For our purposes, the distinction of his utopian projection is that it constituted a kind of transition from the institutional concern of the seventeenth century to the communitarian ideal of the eighteenth and early nineteenth centuries. Fénelon describes two societies, one organized and commercially oriented, the other a simplistic, bucolic society of natural innocence. Fénelon tried to describe the best of both utopian worlds. The emphasis on natural communitarian simplicity was to last for some one hundred and fifty years, during a period in which experiments in the formation of independent, self-sufficient communities became an important ingredient in social and political history, especially in America.

While there remains a considerable interest in the possibility of small communities loosely knit by the supposed precepts of natural law, by the middle of the nineteenth century the great majority of utopists had begun to perceive that the prospects and possibilities in the modern world for the small, isolated, and self-sufficient community were very dim and unpromising. The age of industrialization, of urban growth, and of technology presented a historical inexorability which few utopists could ignore. Utopian writing reflects this recognition, and there was a revival of concern for institutional structures which would confer the benefits of production and distribution upon men in a more equable and utopian fashion. Edward Bellamy was certainly the outstanding example of this nineteenth century optimism about a future centralized and industrialized society. It seems generally to have been ignored that many of the utopists of this period, including Bellamy, were much concerned with the problem of city planning and urban organization; one of the earliest of these was Mary Griffith (1836). There is little present evidence that the utopist's foreknowledge bore appreciable fruit.

The generalized hope and expectation of the late nineteenth century utopists were shattered by the traumatic impact of World War I on an apparently unsuspecting Western society. The potential achievements and benefits of governments and industry became instead instruments of death, destruction, and a flight from utopia. It could only be expected that the period following such a devastating destruction of utopian ideals would produce an unparalleled preponderance of dystopian writings. Satires, burlesques, and dire predictions concerning every institutional structure from economics to government to religion and education prevailed in utopian writing; to some considerable extent they are still a dominant theme of the literature today. Yet ideals and dreams persist in the minds of men, and the great and fascinating tradition and history of utopian speculation will continue to be enriched by the writings of these idealists.

UTOPIAN LITERATURE

Influence

An assessment of the influence of utopists and their writings is unquestionably most difficult to make. In a few instances some documentation can be found to support a claim of direct or indirect influence, but these are the exceptions. More's *Utopia,* for example, undoubtedly stimulated utopian thought and provided a model for much utopian construction. On the other hand, it is questionable what actual influence *Utopia* had on social and political developments, partly because just what More meant to convey or suggest remains a matter of moot scholarly appraisal.

The influence of Edward Bellamy is well attested and documented, in economic thought and especially in the Populist movement in the United States. The number of utopian works in imitation, extenuation, or criticism of *Looking Backward* is evidence of his widespread influence. The very significant impact of James Harrington on subsequent political development, especially on the structure of the Constitution of the United States, is a matter of undeniable documentary evidence, but for some strange reason the profound and enduring effect of Harrington's utopian ideals on American thought and politics has been almost totally neglected in histories and analyses of the eighteenth century and the birth of the United States.[6] It is surprising that the republican Harrington was so much influenced by his observation of the government of Venice; likely he was also acquainted with the work of Contarini on that subject. Whatever the sources of his thought, certainly his ideals as expressed in his utopia were to have a lasting effect on the political histories of the United States and England: the ballot as statutory method of election; an elected senate and popular assembly; abolishment of primogeniture; limitation of ownership of property.

There is an almost irresistible urge on the part of anyone immersed in utopian literature to attribute the stature and influence of an author to his utopian writing. In most cases that would be a mistaken judgment, for, more often than not, it is the utopian work which is least known and most neglected. Prudence dictates the "is," for judgment of how well known and how influential some of these utopian works were in their own day awaits more intensive and concerned research than has thus far been evident in most appraisals of utopist authors.

Some other examples of the influence of utopists' ideals on the thought of their world could be cited, but for the most part the influence of the

---

[6] See Charles Blitzler, *An Immortal Commonwealth* (New Haven, 1960); Zera Fink, *The Classical Republicans* (Evanston, Ill., 1945); and H. F. Russell-Smith, *Harrington and His Oceana* (Cambridge, 1914).

Introduction

utopists must now be judged on the rather tenuous grounds of the number of printings, editions, and translations which their works achieved. Any effort to list all such editions and translations in this bibliography would be both tedious and unrewarding; but even a brief perusal of the catalogues in any of the libraries listed will, in a surprising number of cases, reveal a record of reprintings and translations that, in consideration of the literate population of the sixteenth, seventeenth, and eighteenth centuries particularly, is truly astonishing. It is not a wild or unreasonable surmise, therefore, to accept the inference that such utopian writings had a significant impact on the thought and the literature of at least their own times.

Further research in utopian literature, its authors, and their influence—the encouragement and facilitation of which is the primary purpose of this bibliography—will without doubt reveal unsuspected effects of utopists on both political philosophy and literary history.

AUTHORS

The authorship of utopian literature is, not unexpectedly, as wide-ranging as is its content—from the illiterate (Sagean) to the most sophisticated and notable figures of literature, philosophy, and science in the Western world. The number of contributors from finance and industry is rather impressive, as is the fact that more than sixty women used this form to express their views.

One of the astonishing instances of neglect in the literature, as has been noted above, is the lack of attention to utopian works by some of the world's most distinguished and widely read authors; to avoid a long catalogue of such personages, a few may be noted: Defoe, Butler, Disraeli, Goldsmith, France, Graves, Lytton, Madariaga, Morris, Clemens, Trollope. Commentaries on the authors and their collected works quite often ignore these utopian speculations, which surely should be very important in any assessment of the author. For example, there is something rather startling in a comparison of the idyllic, romantic picture of Percy Bysshe Shelley's *The Assassins* (1816), written shortly after his elopement with Mary Wollstonecraft Godwin to Switzerland, and the grim, dystopian story *The Last Man* (1826) written by her four years after his death. I have never found *The Fixed Period* in any collected works of Anthony Trollope, yet it is today a more relevant, if bitter, anticipation of the controversy about euthanasia than when it was written in 1882.

There are a number of surprising authors of utopian speculation and fantasy. The Marquis de Sade wrote a most bucolic and arcadian romance, *Aline et Valcour;* Edward Mandell House, intimate adviser to President

Woodrow Wilson, offered a distressing anticipation of the future necessity for a military dictator (temporary, of course) in *Phillip Dru: Administrator* (1912); John Jacob Astor and King Camp Gillette are examples of business tycoons who sought expression of their ideals in utopian construction.

SCIENCE FICTION

The field of science fiction, which has so recently achieved scholarly respectability, presents an insuperable bibliographic problem. In the first place, it is almost impossible for one person to become acquainted with all the writing in this burgeoning and prolific medium, much less to do so and also to maintain acquaintance with utopian literature as such. The problem has intensified recently; from the time of classical literature there have been outstanding examples of so-called science fiction, and some of these works have been included here (*e.g.*, by Defoe, Cyrano de Bergerac, Greg, Coblentz) because they also fit our definition of utopian structure. An analysis of contemporary science fiction to determine what works might meet the definitive qualifications of utopian speculation would be a monumental task, one possible only by the combined efforts of a number of persons.[7] Therefore, it is with some apology that it must be admitted that the present bibliography may indeed neglect works of science fiction which should have been included.

"UTOPIAN" COMMUNITIES

The generic use of *utopian* to designate the great number of communitarian enterprises in America, especially from 1700 to 1850, is understandable but misleading. In only one instance among more than one hundred and fifty such experiments was the structure of the society the result of the inspiration and influence of a utopia as we have defined that genre for the purposes of this bibliography; the exception was the extensive, tenacious, and

---

[7] The most ambitious effort to present in a meaningful way this vast expanse of literature is that of Pierre Versins, *Encyclopédie de l'Utopie, des Voyages Extraordinaires, et de la Science Fiction* (Lausanne, 1972), 997 pages, profusely illustrated. The work does not include most of the lesser known items of utopian literature and is understandably very limited in reference to British and American authors. Nevertheless, Versins's acquaintance is indeed almost encyclopedic, and his editorial remarks are delightful, such as his comments on the long abortive Icarian experiments in America: *"Le métier d'utopiste est dur."*

Introduction

courageous Icarian movement in America which struggled for one hundred years to realize the communitarian ideals so optimistically and naively proclaimed in Étienne Cabet's *Voyage en Icarie.* Cabet's report on the *Colonie Icarienne aux États-Unis d'Amerique* is the only reference in the following bibliography to "utopian" communities.

This omission is a matter of definitive rather than value judgment; such colonies as New Harmony, Oneida, Amana, Brook Farm, the Fourier phalansteries, and others were not the result of any influence of utopian literature. Indeed, in the records of these communities and the comments about them, there is a surprising absence of any reference to utopian writers or literature according to our definition used here.[8]

Notation

The purpose of this bibliography could hardly have been accomplished by an examination of one or two libraries because many of the items are quite rare; nor was it feasible to examine a large number of libraries with limited holdings of titles. Therefore, eleven libraries were selected on the basis of their extensive listings of works and on the basis of their geographical locations in order to facilitate their use by scholars.

Any attempt to list numbers of editions and translations would contribute confusion rather than clarity to the intent of this bibliography; such details as publisher, imprimatur, and questionable dates of issue are of great interest to the bibliophile-collector, but of little concern to those interested in the content and influence of the work. In very few instances is there any substantial difference between editions, and while translations naturally differ, there is usually little difference of importance. Even the Russian translation of More's *Utopia,* as used in Stalin's U.S.S.R., withstands scrutiny for the validity of the translation. Thus, only those editions and translations which are of particular significance or which are accessible in the libraries listed have been included. Important works which are available in translation have been noted; for example, if a work in English has been translated into French, it will be listed: BN (French). A few very rare items have been listed in other libraries: for example, Biblioteca Nacional, Madrid.

---

[8] The classic commentary on these communitarian experiments, since it was based on personal observation, is that of Charles Nordhoff, *The Communist Societies of the United States* (New York, 1875; New York, 1965). See also: Arthur E. Bestor, *Backwoods Utopias* (Philadelphia, 1950); Mark Holloway, *Heavens on Earth* (New York, 1966); and Peyton E. Richter, *Utopias: Social Ideals and Communal Experiments* (Boston, 1971).

The title listed is that of the original edition insofar as it is known. In many instances, there is some variation in the titles of later editions.

The date is that of the original edition insofar as it is known.

The listing for libraries is that of the earliest known edition in each library; other editions may be checked in the catalogues. The availability of every book in every library listed can hardly be a matter of assurance and is subject to change; the frustration of receiving call slips stamped with "Cannot Be Located," "Lost," or "Misplaced" must occasionally be expected.

In this important matter of availability, the Utopia Collection of the Duke University Library is distinguished in the fact that it is housed, as a collection, in the Rare Book Room of that library. It would be an unusual exception if any work listed in the Utopia Collection is not immediately available for use by resident or visiting scholars.

The cross reference of pseudonyms and alternative names is a tiresome but necessary interpolation in the listing. In perhaps no other literature were so many works published anonymously or under pseudonyms, and in a surprising number of libraries cataloguing may still be by pseudonym or alternate name. It is suggested, therefore, that in the search for some works listed, it may be necessary to check under name, alternate name, pseudonym, or title. The first edition of Sinold's *Die Glückseeligste Insul,* for example, is listed by the British Museum under Constantinus von Wahrenberg, for some inexplicable reason, although later editions are properly catalogued.

A most significant concern for scholarly research in the field of utopian literature is the availability of the works; some of them are very rare. One of the primary purposes of this bibliography is to provide a listing of libraries in which utopian items can be located. Few scholars, however, can afford the time and expense necessary to explore eleven libraries widely scattered across the United States, England, and France. Therefore, the problem of obtaining copies of otherwise unavailable works is of extreme importance—for example, if one were to contemplate an analysis of utopian thought in eighteenth century France. If information about the availability of photostat or microfilm copies were reliable, it would be most pertinent to include such directions here as an assistance to research. Unfortunately this cannot be done; especially with the present ambiguity about copyright privileges, the policies of various libraries in supplying copies of works are so variable and changing that any effort to list those policies would be confusing rather than helpful.

Library Locations

BM	British Museum, London
BN	Bibliothèque Nationale, Paris
Bod	Bodleian Library, Oxford
CSmH	Huntington Library, San Marino, California
CtY	Yale University, New Haven, Connecticut
DLC	Library of Congress, Washington, D.C.
ICN	Newberry Library, Chicago, Illinois
ICU	University of Chicago, Chicago, Illinois
MH	Harvard University, Cambridge, Massachusetts
NcD	The Glenn Negley Utopia Collection, Duke University, Durham, North Carolina
NN	New York City Public Library

A few particularly rare items are given a special listing, e.g., Biblioteca Nacional, Madrid.

A Bibliography
of Utopian Literature

A Bibliography

1   Abbott, Leonard Dalton, 1878–.
    The Society of the Future. Girard, Kan., 1898. 111 p.

    BM NN

2   *An Account of Count d'Artois and His Friend's Passage to the Moon
    . . . Giving an Account of . . . the Inhabitants; their Language,
    Manners, Religion, etc.* Litchfield, Conn., 1785. 32 p. (Copy-
    right July 20, 1785, by Daniel Moore.)

    CtY (film)   DLC (photostat)

3   Achá. *See* Aguirre Achá, José.

4   Acherley, Roger, 1665(?)–1740.
    *The Britannic Constitution: or, The Fundamental Form of
    Government in Britain. Demonstrating, the Original Contract
    Entered into by King and People According to the Primary
    Institutions Thereof, in This Nation.* London, 1727. 695 p.

    BM BN CSmH ICN NcD   1741: CtY DLC MH NN

5   ————.

    *Reasons for Uniformity in the State. Being a Supplement to the
    Britannic Constitution.* London, 1741. 59 p.

    BM BN CtY DLC ICN MH   1780: CSmH

6   Adam, Paul Auguste Marie, 1862–1920.
    Lettres de Malaisie; Roman. Paris, 1897. 238 p.

    BN   1898: BM DLC MH NcD NN

7   ————.

    La Cité Prochaine. Lettres de Malaisie. Paris, 1908. 279 p.

    BM BN

8   ————.

    La Ville Inconnue. Paris, 1911. 446 p.

    BM BN CtY DLC MH NcD

9   Adams, Francis (*pseud.*). *See* Cabet, Étienne.

3

10   Adams, Frederick Upham, 1859–1921.
President John Smith: the Story of a Peaceful Revolution. Chicago, 1897. 289 p. (First published in serial form in the *Chicago Times*.)
CSmH CtY DLC ICN ICU NcD NN

11   Adams, J. (*pseud.* Skelton Kuppord).
The Unchartered Island. London, 1899. 350 p.
BM NN

12   ————.
A Fortune from the Sky. London, 1903. 230 p.
BM MH NcD

13   Adams, Jack (*pseud.*). *See* Grigsby, Alcanoan O.

14   Adderley, James Granville, 1861–.
Stephen Remarx; the Story of a Venture in Ethics. London, 1893. 150 p.
BM DLC   1894: ICU MH NcD NN

15   Affricano, Raoul.
Una Visita Inaspettata, Avventura Inverosimile. Rome, 1938. 22 p.
NN

16   Agostini, Ludovico, 1536–1612.
La Repubblica Immaginaria. Testo Critico, con la Bibliografia dell'Autore, a Cura di Luigi Firpo. Turin, 1957. 187 p. (Probably written *ca.* 1583–1590.)
BM BN DLC ICN ICU NcD NN

17   Aguilar, Maximiliano.
Feria de Repúblicas. Buenos Aires, 1947. 440 p.
CtY DLC ICU NN

18   Aguirre Achá, José (Achá), 1877–.
Platonia, Escenas de la Democracia en la América Latina; Novela Política. La Paz, 1923. 435 p.
BM DLC ICU NcD NN

4

A Bibliography

19 d'Alais. *See* Vairasse, Denis.

20 Alexander, James Bradun, 1831–.
    The Lunarian Professor and His Remarkable Revelations Concerning the Earth, the Moon and Mars, Together with an Account of the Cruise of the Sally Ann. Minneapolis, 1909. 291 p.
    CtY DLC NcD NN

21 Allais. *See* Vairasse, Denis.

22 Allen, Charles Grant Blairfindie (Grant Allen), 1848–1899.
    The British Barbarians. New York and London, 1895. 281 p.
    BM CtY DLC ICN ICU MH NcD NN

23 ————.
    "The Child of the Phalanstery." In *Twelve Tales,* chap. 3. London, 1899.
    BM DLC MH NcD

24 [Allen, Henry Francis] (*pseud.* Pruning Knife).
    The Key of Industrial Co-operative Government. St. Louis, 1886. 133 p.
    DLC NN

25 [————].
    A Strange Voyage. A Revision of The Key of Industrial Co-operative Government. An Interesting and Instructive Description of Life on Planet Venus. St. Louis, 1891. 226 p.
    CtY DLC

26 Altair (*pseud.*). *See* Griffin, Anthony Jerome.

27 Alterego (*pseud.*). *See* Jaffe, Hyman.

28 Amersin, Ferdinand.
    Das Land der Freiheit. Ein Zukunftsbild in Schlichter Erzählungsform. 346 p. (Vol. 2 of *Weisheit und Tugend des Reinen Menschenthums.* Graz, 1871, 1874.)
    BM BN DLC MH

5

29   Ammon, M.
      Das Ei des Kolumbus, Sozialer Roman. Leipzig, 1909. 432 p.
      DLC

30   Andreä, Johann Valentin, 1586–1654.
      Reipublicae Christianopolitanae Descriptio. Argentorati (i.e.,
      Strasbourg), 1619. 220 p.
      BM BN CtY DLC MH   1633: ICU

31   —————.
      Christianopolis; an Ideal State of the Seventeenth Century.
      Translated by Felix Emil Held. New York, 1916. 287 p.
      BM BN CtY DLC ICN ICU MH NcD NN

32   Anson, August.
      When Woman Reigns. Oxford, 1938. 205 p.
      BM

33   *Antangil. See* M., I. D., G. T.

34   *Antéaur.* Paris, 1929. 206 p. (Preface signed "Antehus.")
      BN DLC

35   *Anticipation. See Private Letters.*

36   *Antiquity Reviv'd, or the Government of a Certain Island Antiently
      Call'd Astreada, in Reference to Religion, Policy, War, and
      Peace; Some Hundreds of Years Before the Coming of Christ.*
      London, 1693. 126 p. (Sometimes catalogued *Astreada.*)
      BM Bod CtY NN

37   [Arcq, Philippe Auguste de Sainte-Foix, chevalier d'], 1721–1779.
      Lettres d'Osman. 3 vols. in 1. Constantinople (i.e., Paris), 1753.
      BM BN NcD   1756: NN   1779: ICU

38   Ardrey, Robert, 1908–.
      Worlds Beginning. New York, 1944. 244 p.
      CtY DLC ICN ICU MH NcD NN   1945: BM

A Bibliography

39   Armstrong, Charles Wicksteed, 1871–.
      *Paradise Found; or, Where the Sex Problem Has Been Solved
      (a Story from South America).* London, 1936. 211 p.
      BM BN CtY DLC

40   [Armstrong, Charles Wicksteed] (*pseud.* Charles Strongi'th'arm),
      1871–.
      *The Yorl of the Northmen; or, the Fate of the English Race.
      Being the Romance of a Monarchical Utopia.* London, 1892.
      127 p.
      BM

41   Armstrong, Capt. Jacob D. (*pseud.*). *See* Meeker, Nathan Cook.

42   Arnold, Birch (*pseud.*). *See* Bartlett, Mrs. Alice Elinor (Bowen).

43   Arrivabene, Lodovico.
      *Il Magno Vitei. In Questo Libro, Oltre al Piacere, che Porge la
      Narratione della Alte Cavallerie del Glorioso Vitei Primo Re
      della China, & del Valoroso Iolao, Si ha Nella Persona de
      Ezonlum, uno Ritratto di Ottimo Prencipe, & di Capitano
      Perfetto.* Verona, 1597. 526 p.
      BM BN ICN NcD NN   1599: DLC

44   [Artus, Thomas, Sieur d'Embry.]
      Les Hermaphrodites à Tous [*L'Île des Hermaphrodites Nou-
      vellement Déscouverte*]. N.p., 1605. 202 p. (*See* Petit de
      Bretigny, Jonathas.)
      BM BN MH   1724: DLC   1726: NcD   1744: ICN

45   Ashbee, Charles Robert, 1863–1942.
      The Building of Thelema. London, 1910. 361 p.
      BM

46   Askham, Francis (*pseud.*). *See* Greenwood, Julia Eileen Courtney.

47   Astor, John Jacob, 1864–1912.
      A Journey in Other Worlds. A Romance of the Future. New
      York, 1894. 476 p.
      BM BN CSmH CtY DLC ICN ICU MH NcD NN

48 *Astreada.* See *Antiquity Reviv'd.*

49 Atkins, John Alfred, 1916–.
Tomorrow Revealed. London, 1955. 254 p.
BM DLC NcD NN   1956: MH   1958 (French): BN

50 Atlas, Martin.
Die Befreiung; ein Zukunftsroman. Berlin, 1910. 475 p.
DLC

51 Atterbom, Per Daniel Amadeus, 1790–1855.
Lycksalighetens Ö Sagospel i Fem Äfventyr. 2 vols. Upsala, 1824–27.
BM MH   1875: NcD   1903: NN   1927: ICU
1945: ICN   1957 (abridged): DLC

52 Atterley, Joseph (*pseud.*). *See* Tucker, George.

53 Auletes, Grazianus Agricola. *See* Pfeiffer, Johann Gregor.

54 [Austen, Edward J.]
The Lost Island: with a Conclusion by W. L. Garrison. New York, 1892. 35 p.
CtY NN   1897: MH

55 Authwise, Eugene (*pseud.?*).
"Ultrawa." *Overland Monthly* 9, 10, 11 (1872–73).
BM CtY DLC ICN ICU MH NcD NN

56 Bacas, Paul Edmond.
Thirty Years to Win. Rindge, N.H., 1954. 209 p.
DLC NcD NN

57 [Bachelder, John.]
A.D. 2050: Electrical Development at Atlantis. By a Former Resident of "The Hub." San Francisco, 1890. 83 p.
CSmH DLC ICN NcD NN

58   [Bachstrom, Johann Friedrich], 1686–1742.
Das bey Zwey Hundert Jahr Lang Unbekannte, Nunmehro aber Entdeckte Vortreffliche Land der Inquiraner. 2 vols. Frankfurt and Leipzig, 1736.

University of Michigan, Ann Arbor, Mich.

59   Bacon, Sir Francis, baron Verulam, viscount St. Albans, 1561–1626.
New Atlantis, a Worke Unfinished. London, 1627. 47 p.
[Bound with *Sylva Sylvarum.* Catalogued variously as 1626 and 1627, *New Atlantis* was probably written 1612–13 (E. A. Abbott), certainly before 1617 (S. R. Gardiner).]

BM CSmH CtY ICN MH   1628: DLC
1631: ICU NcD   1635: BN   1643: NN

60   Bacon, Samuels (*pseud.*). *See* Samuels, Philip Francis.

61   Ball, Frank P.
My Wondrous Dream. New York, 1923. 182 p.

CtY DLC ICU MH NN

62   Ballanche, Pierre Simon, 1776–1847.
La Ville des Expiations, Trois Épisodes. Paris, 1832. 24 p.

BN

63   ————.
La Ville des Expiations (Livres IV à VII). Edited by A. Rastoul. Paris, 1926. 136 p.

BN CtY DLC ICN ICU NcD NN

64   [Balthazard, abbé], *d.* 1801.
L'Îsle des Philosophes et Plusieurs Autres, Nouvellement Découvertes, & Remarquables par Leurs Rapports avec la France Actuelle. Chartres, 1790. 340 p.

BN DLC

65   Barlow, James William, 1826–1913.
The Immortals' Great Quest: Translated from an Unpublished Manuscript in the Library of a Continental University. London, 1909. 177 p.

BM NcD

[This delightful little work was first published as *History of a World of Immortals without a God* (Dublin, 1891), under the pseudonym Antares Skorpios. Both Stillwell and Halkett & Laing erroneously attributed the pseudonym to James Barlow's daughter, Jane Barlow, a widely read Irish poetess. The two editions are identical except for some changes of quotation marks. The only copy found of the first edition is in the Bodleian Library, catalogued under Jane Barlow (photostat in Duke Library).]

66　Barnes, Joshua, 1654–1712.
　　Gerania; a New Discovery of a Little Sort of People Anciently Discoursed of, Called Pygmies. London, 1675. 110 p.

　　BM BN Bod CSmH DLC ICN ICU MH NcD NN
　　1750: CtY

67　Barrière, Marcel, 1861–.
　　[*La Dernière Épopée.*] *Le Monde Noir. Roman sur l'Avenir des Sociétés Humaines.* Paris, 1909. 430 p.

　　BN DLC NcD　　1911: NN

68　Bart-Claye, A.
　　Vers la Cité Future. Paris, 1905. 168 p.

　　BN

69　[Bartlett, Mrs. Alice Elinor (Bowen)] (*pseud.* Birch Arnold), 1848–1920.
　　A New Aristocracy. New York and Detroit, 1891. 316 p.

　　BM DLC NcD

70　Bayne, Charles Joseph, 1870–.
　　The Fall of Utopia. Boston, 1900. 190 p.

　　CSmH DLC ICN MH NcD NN

71　[Beaconsfield, Benjamin Disraeli, 1st earl of], 1804–1881.
　　The Voyage of Captain Popanilla. London, 1828. 243 p.

　　BM CSmH CtY DLC ICN ICU MH NcD NN
　　Works: BN

72   Beaujon, Paul (*pseud.*). *See* Warde, Beatrice Lamberton (Becker).

73   [Beffroy de Reigny, Louis Abel] (*pseud.* Cousin-Jacques), 1757–1811.
    Nicodème dans la Lune, ou, la Révolution Pacifique. Folie en Prose et en Trois Actes. Paris, 1791. 72 p.

    BM BN DLC MH NcD

74   [————].
    La Constitution de la Lune, Rêve Politique et Moral. Par le Cousin-Jacques. Paris, 1793. 302 p.

    BM BN CtY ICN NcD NN

75   *The Beginning; a Romance of Chicago as It Might Be.* Chicago, 1893.

    CtY MH

76   Behn, Mrs. Aphra (Amis), 1640–1689.
    [The] Emperor of the Moon: a Farce. London, 1687. 67 p.
    BM CSmH CtY ICU MH NN   1688: DLC ICN NcD

77   Bélin. *See* Béllin de la Liborlière.

78   Bell, George W.
    Mr. Oseba's Last Discovery. Wellington, N.Z., 1904. 225 p.
    CtY DLC ICN ICU MH NcD NN

79   Bell, Neill (*pseud.*). *See* Southwold, Stephen.

80   Bellamy, Edward, 1850–1898.
    Looking Backward, 2000–1887. Boston, 1888. 470 p.

    BM CSmH CtY DLC ICN MH NcD NN
    1889: ICU   n.d.: BN

81   ————.
    Equality. New York, 1897. 412 p.

    BM CSmH CtY DLC ICN MH NcD NN

82 Béllin de la Liborlière, Louis François Marie (Bélin; La Liborlière), 1774–1847.
Voyage de M. Candide Fils au Pays d'Eldorado, Vers la Fin du Dix-Huitième Siècle; pour Servir de Suite aux Aventures de M. son Père. Paris, 1803. 224 p.

BN CtY MH NcD

83 Benefice (*pseud.*). *See* Worley, Frederick U.

84 Benitez de Castro, Cecilio, 1917–.
Los Dias Están Contados. Barcelona, 1944. 254 p.

DLC ICU

85 Bennett, Richard M. *See* Hicks, Granville.

86 Benson, Ramsey (*pseud.*). *See* Ramsey, Percival.

87 Benson, Robert Hugh, 1871–1914.
Lord of the World. London, 1907. 384 p.

BM ICN NcD   1908: CtY DLC MH   1915: NN
1908 (French): BN

88 ―――――.
The Dawn of All. St. Louis, 1911. 423 p. London, 1911. 339 p.

BM DLC ICN MH NcD   1915 (French): BN

89 [Berens, Lewis Henry and Ignatius Singer.]
The Story of My Dictatorship. New York, 1894. 48 p.

CSmH   1910: BM NN   191–: ICU   1934: DLC
n.d.: CtY NcD

90 Beresford, John Davys, 1873–1947.
Goslings. A World of Women. London, 1913. 325 p.

BM CSmH CtY DLC ICU NcD NN

91 ―――――.
Revolution; a Story of the Near Future in England. London, 1921. 252 p.

BM CSmH CtY DLC MH NcD NN

92   Beresford, Leslie (*pseud.* Pan).
       The Kingdom of Content. London, 1918. 278 p.

       BM

93   [Berington, Simon], 1680–1755.
       The Memoirs of Sigr. Guadentio di Lucca: Taken from His Confession and Examination Before the Fathers of the Inquisition. London, 1737. 335 p.

       BM DLC ICN ICU NcD NN   1748: CtY
       1798: CSmH

94   Il Bernia (*pseud.*). *See* Teluccini, Mario.

95   Besant, Sir Walter, 1836–1901.
       All Sorts and Conditions of Men; an Impossible Story. 3 vols. London, 1882. (New York, 1882. 82 p. With James Rice.)

       BM BN CSmH CtY DLC MH NcD NN   1889: ICN
       1896: ICU

96   ————.
       The Revolt of Man. Edinburgh, 1882. 358 p.

       BM CtY DLC MH NN   1896: NcD

97   ————.
       The Inner House. Bristol and London, 1888. 198 p.

       BM CSmH CtY DLC MH NcD NN

98   ————.
       Ivory Gate. 3 vols. London, 1892. (New York, 1892. 359 p.)

       BM BN CSmH CtY DLC ICU MH NcD

99   Best, Herbert.
       The Twenty-Fifth Hour. New York, 1940. 321 p.

       BM CtY DLC NcD NN

100   Béthune, le chevalier de.
       Relation du Monde de Mercure. Geneva, 1750. 286 p.

       BM BN CtY ICN NcD   1787: CSmH NN

101   Bettauer, Hugo, 1872–1925.
Die Stadt Ohne Juden. Ein Roman von Übermorgen. Vienna
and Leipzig, 1924. 217 p.

BM   1929 (French): BN

102   ————.
The City Without Jews; a Novel of Our Time. Translated by
S. N. Brainin. New York, 1926. 189 p.

BM CtY DLC MH NcD NN

103   [Bettinelli, Saverio], 1718–1808.
Il Mondo della Luna. Venice, 1754. 266 p.

BN NcD

104   Bevington, Louisa Sarah.
Common Sense Country. London, 189–. 12 p.

NcD

105   Bikkers, Alexander V. W. (*pseud.*). *See* Harting, Pieter.

106   Bilz, Friedrich Eduard, 1842–1922.
*Der Zukunftsstaat. Staatseinrichtung im Jahre 2000; Neue
Weltanschauung. Jedermann Wird ein Glückliches und Sor-
genfreies dasein Gesichtert.* Leipzig, 1904. 886 p.

DLC ICN   1905: DLC   1905 (French): BN

107   ————.
In Hundert Jahren; Reich Illustrierter Roman. Leipzig, 1907.
1132 p.

DLC ICN

108   Bird, Arthur.
*Looking Forward. A Dream of the United States of the Ameri-
cas in 1999.* Utica, N.Y., 1899. 234 p.

MH NcD NN

109   Birkenhead, Frederick Edwin Smith, earl of, 1872–1930.
The World in 2030 A.D. London, 1930. 215 p.

BM CtY DLC ICN MH NcD NN

110   Bischoff, Diedrich, 1866–.
       Masonia; ein Blick in eine Andere Welt. Leipzig, 1905.
       Cornell University, Ithaca, N.Y.

111   ————.
       Heimat; eine Botschaft vom Neuen Vaterland. Leipzig, 1924.
       333 p.
       DLC NN

112   Bishop, William Henry, 1843–1928.
       The Garden of Eden, U.S.A.; a Very Possible Story. Chicago,
       1895. 369 p.
       CtY DLC NN

113   [Blair, Andrew, M.D.]
       *Annals of the Twenty-Ninth Century; or, the Autobiography
       of the Tenth President of the World Republic.* 3 vols. London,
       1874.
       BM

114   [Blair, Eric Arthur] (*pseud.* George Orwell), 1903–1950.
       Animal Farm. London, 1945. 91 p.
       BM CSmH DLC ICU MH NcD   1946: CtY NN
       1953: ICN   n.d.: BN

115   [————].
       Nineteen Eighty-Four. London, 1949. 312 p.
       BM CSmH CtY DLC ICN ICU MH NcD NN
       n.d.: BN

116   Blanchard, Charles Elton, M.D., 1868–.
       *A New Day Dawns; a Brief History of the Altruistic Era
       (1930-2162 A.D.) A.E. 200.* Youngstown, Ohio, 1932. 191 p.
       DLC ICU MH NcD NN

117   Blatchford, Robert, 1851–1943.
       The Sorcery Shop: An Impossible Romance. London, 1907.
       199 p.
       BM ICN NcD NN

118   Blot, Thomas (*pseud.*). *See* Simpson, William.

119   Boccalini, Traiano, 1556–1613.
    De' Ragguagli di Parnaso . . . Centuria prima. Venice, 1612.
    478 p.
    BM ICN ICU NcD   1613: Cty   1614: BN MH NN
    1617: DLC   1624: CSmH

120   ——————.
    . . . Centuria seconda. Venice, 1613. 453 p.
    BM ICN   1614: BN NcD NN   1617: DLC

121   ——————.
    *Pietra del Paragone Politico Tratta dal Monte Parnaso, Dove si
    Toccano i Governi delle Maggiori Monarchie dell'Universo.*
    Cormopoli (Venice?), 1615. 138 p.
    BM BN CtY DLC ICN MH   1671: CSmH
    1675: NcD   1863: ICU NN

122   ——————.
    Ragguagli di Parnaso. Edited by Luigi Firpo. 3 vols. Bari, 1948.
    BM CtY DLC ICN MH NcD

123   ——————.
    The New-Found Politicke. Translated by John Florio, Thomas
    Scott and Sir William Vaughan. London, 1626. 242 p.
    BM CSmH CtY DLC ICU MH NN

124   ——————.
    *I Ragguagli di Parnaso: or, Advertisements from Parnassus.
    With the Politick Touchstone . . . Now Put into English by
    the Right Honorable, Henry, Earl of Monmouth.* London,
    1656. 452 p.
    BM CSmH DLC ICN ICU MH   1669: NcD NN

125   ——————.
    *Advices from Parnassus, in Two Centuries, with the Political
    Touchstone. Revis'd and Corrected by Mr. Hughes.* London,
    1706. 454 p.
    BM CSmH DLC ICN ICU MH NcD

126   Boisgilbert, Edmund, M.D. (*pseud.*). *See* Donnelly, Ignatius.

127   Bond, Frederick Bligh, 1864–.
       *The Hill of Vision; a Forecast of the Great War and of Social
       Revolution with the Coming of the New Race, Gathered from
       Automatic Writings Obtained Between 1909 and 1912, and
       Also, in 1918.* Boston, 1919. 134 p.

       BM CtY DLC ICN MH NcD NN

128   Bonifacio, Giovanni, 1547–1635.
       *La Republica delle Api . . . con la Quale di Dimostra il Modo di
       Ben Formar un Novo Governo Democratico.* Rovigo, 1627.
       38 p.

       BN   Biblioteca Nacional, Madrid

129   ———.
       *L'Arti Liberali et Mecaniche come Siano State da gli Animali
       Irrationali a gli Huomini Dimostrate.* Rovigo, 1628. 140 p.

       BN   Biblioteca Nacional, Madrid

130   [Bordelon, Laurent], 1653–1730.
       Le Voyage Forcé de Becafort Hypocondriaque. Paris, 1709.
       342 p.

       BM BN CtY DLC ICN NcD

131   Borgese, Elisabeth (Mann).
       "My Own Utopia." In *Ascent of Woman,* epilogue, pp. 209–27.
       New York, 1963.

       BM CtY ICU MH NcD NN

132   [Bougeant, Guillaume Hyacinthe], 1690–1743.
       Voyage Merveilleux du Prince Fan-Férédin dans la Romancie.
       Paris, 1735. 275 p.

       BM BN CtY DLC ICU MH NcD   1738: ICN
       1788: CSmH NN

133   [———].
       *The Wonderful Travels of Prince Fan-Férédin in the Country
       of Arcadia.* Dublin, 1789. 197 p.

       DLC ICN ICU MH

134   Bouic, Frederick Vernon.
        Good-bye, White Man; a Novel of A.D. 2711. New York, 1953.
        241 p.
        DLC NN

135   Bouvé, Edward Tracy.
        Centuries Apart. Boston, 1894. 347 p.
        BM CSmH DLC MH NcD NN

136   Bowhay, Bertha Louisa.
        Elenchus Brown. The Story of an Experimental Utopia Compiled by a Student of Battersea Polytechnic. London, 1929.
        368 p.
        BM NN

137   Bowman, Hildebrand (*pseud.*).
        Travels of Hildebrand Bowman, Esquire, into Carnovirria, Taupiniera, Olfactaria, and Auditante, in New-Zealand; in the Island of Bonhommica, and in the Powerful Kingdom of Luxovolupto, on the Great Southern Continent. London, 1778. 400 p.
        BM CSmH CtY DLC MH NcD

138   Boyle, Capt. Robert (*pseud.*). *See* Chetwood, William Rufus.

139   Brachfeld, Joseph Mauritius von.
        Curieuse und Wunder-volle Begebenheiten in den Unbekannten Sud-Ländern, Nemlich in der Glückseligen Insul Jaketan und dem Unweit Darvon Entlegenen sehr Grossen Reich Adama. Frankfurt and Leipzig, 1739. 682 p.
        BM CtY MH NN

140   Brady, Cyrus Townsend, 1861–1920.
        The Island of Regeneration; a Story of What Ought to Be. New York, 1909. 362 p.
        CtY DLC NN   1910: BM NcD

141   Brant, John Ira, 1872–.
        The New Regime, A.D. 2202. New York and London, 1909.
        122 p.
        BM DLC NcD NN

142   [Brash, Margaret Maud] (*pseud*. John Kendall), 1880–.
       Unborn To-Morrow. London, 1933. 319 p.

       BM Bod DLC NcD   1935 (French): BN

143   Bray, John Francis, 1809–1879.
       A Voyage from Utopia to Several Unknown Regions of the World by Yarbfg. Translated from the American. Edited by M. F. Lloyd-Prichard. London, 1957. 192 p. (Probably written *ca*. 1840–41.)

       BM CtY DLC ICN ICU MH NcD NN

144   Bricaire de la Dixmerie, Nicolas, 1730–1791.
       L'Ísle Taciturne et l'Ísle Enjouée, ou Voyage du Génie Alaciel dans ces Deux Ísles. Amsterdam (i.e., Paris), 1759. 188 p.

       BM BN DLC ICN ICU NcD   1787: NN
       1788: CSmH

145   Brinsmade, Herman Hine.
       Utopia Achieved; a Novel of the Future. New York, 1912. 177 p.

       DLC NcD NN

146   Briusov, Valerii Iakovlevich (Bryusov), 1873–1924.
       "The Republic of the Southern Cross." Chapter 1 in volume of same title, edited by Stephen Graham. London, 1918.

       BM DLC ICU MH NcD

147   Brocardo, Jacopo, *d*. 1594.
       Iacobi Brocardi Libri Duo: Alter ad Christianos de Prophetia. Leyden, 1581. 149 p.

       BM BN

148   ————.
       The Revelation of S. Jhon Reveled, or a Paraphrase Opening by Conference of Time and Place Such Things as Are Both Necessary and Profitable for the Tyme Present. Englished by James Sanford. London, 1582. 170 p.

       BM CSmH ICU

149   Brooks, Byron Alden, 1845–.
       Earth Revisited. Boston, 1893. 318 p.
       BM CSmH NN

150   Brown, Charles Brockden, 1771–1810.
       "Sketches of a History of Carsol." In *The Life of Charles Brockden Brown with Selections . . . from his Manuscripts Before Unpublished,* by William Dunlap, 1: 170–261. Philadelphia, 1815.
       BM CtY DLC ICN ICU MH NcD NN

151   [Brown, John Macmillan] (*pseud.* Godfrey Sweven), 1846–1935.
       Riallaro, the Archipelago of Exiles. London, 1897. 420 p.
       1901: CtY DLC ICN NN   1931: BM MH NcD

152   [————].
       Limanora, the Island of Progress. London and New York. 1903. 711 p.
       BN CtY DLC ICN MH NcD NN   1931: BM

153   Brown, Richard Blake, 1902–.
       A Broth of a Boy. London, 1933. 373 p.
       BM NcD

154   Browne, Maurice and Harold Edward Monro.
       Proposals for a Voluntary Nobility. Norwich, Eng., 1907. 31 p.
       BM

155   *Bruce's Voyage to Naples and Journey up Mount Vesuvius; Giving an Account of the Discovery of the Central World; with the Laws, Customs and Manners of the Nation Described.* London, 1802.
       Bod

156   Bruno, Giordano, 1548–1600.
       Spaccio de la Bestia Trionfante, Proposto da Giove, Effettuato dal Conseglo, Revelato da Mercurio, Recitato da Sophia. Parigi (i.e., London), 1584. 261 p.
       BM BN CtY MH   1830: NcD   1863: CSmH ICU
       1888: DLC ICN NN

157   ——————.

Spaccio della Bestia Trionfante. Or the Expulsion of the Tri-umphant Beast. Translated by William Morehead. London, 1713. 280 p.

BM BN CSmH CtY

158   ——————.

The Expulsion of the Triumphant Beast. Translated by Arthur D. Imerti. New Brunswick, N.J., 1964. 324 p.

Bod CtY ICN ICU MH NcD NN

159   Brunt, Samuel (*pseud.*).
A Voyage to Cacklogallinia: with a Description of the Religion, Policy, Customs and Manners of That Country. London, 1727. 167 p.

BM CSmH CtY ICN MH

160   ——————.

A Voyage. . . . Edited by M. Nicolson. New York, 1940. 167 p.

BM CSmH CtY DLC ICN ICU MH NcD NN

161   Bryusov. *See* Briusov.

162   [Buchan, John, 1875–1940, and Susan, 1882–] (*pseuds.* Cadmus and Harmonia).
The Island of Sheep. London, 1919. 193 p.

BM   1920: DLC MH NcD NN

163   Buchanan, Robert Williams, 1841–1901.
The Rev. Annabel Lee. A Tale of To-morrow. London, 1898. 255 p.

BM CSmH ICN MH

164   Bulwer-Lytton. *See* Lytton, Edward George Earle Bulwer.

165   Buonamico, Matteo, *d.* 1590.
Trattato della Servitu . . . Volontaria, nel Quale Moralmente di Discorre della Vita di Chiunque Serve. Naples, 1572. 173 p.

Bod   1581: BN   1590: BM

166   ———.

"L'Isola di Narsida." In *Utopisti Italiani del Cinquecento,* edited by Carlo Curcio, pp. 173-93. Rome, 1944.

ICN ICU

167   Burgess, Anthony *(pseud.)*. *See* Wilson, John Anthony Burgess.

168   [Burgh, James] *(pseud.* J. Vander Neck), 1714–1775.

An Account of the First Settlement, Laws, Form of Government, and Police, of the Cessares, a People of South America: in Nine Letters, from Mr. Vander Neck, One of the Senators of that Nation, to His Friend in Holland. London, 1764. 121 p.

BM CtY DLC ICN MH NN

169   [Burton, Robert] *(pseud.* Democritus, Junior), 1577–1640.

"An Utopia of Mine Own." A part of the preface to *The Anatomy of Melancholy.* Oxford, 1621. (This brief but significant little piece was expanded gradually in later editions.)

BM CSmH CtY DLC ICN MH   1624: NN
1632: ICU   1638: BN NcD

170   Busens, Sieur de.

Histoire du Royaume des Amans, avec les Loix et les Coustumes que les Peuples y Observent et leur Origine du Pais des Amadis. Toulouse, 1666. 104 p.

BN CtY

171   Butler, Samuel, 1835–1902.

Erewhon; or, Over the Range. London, 1872. 246 p.

BM CSmH CtY ICN MH NcD   1873: NN
1910: DLC   1917: ICU   n.d.: BN

172   ———.

Erewhon Revisited Twenty Years Later, Both by the Original Discoverer of the Country and by His Son. London, 1901. 338 p.

BM CSmH CtY ICN MH NcD   1910: ICU NN
1916: DLC   n.d.: BN

173   C., C.
      *The Father of the City of Eutopia, or the Surest Road to Riches.
      Being a Narrative of the Remarkable Life and Adventures of an
      Elevated Bear* [*sic*], *etc. Delivered Under the Similitude of a
      Dream.* London, 1757. 22 p.

      BM CtY

174   [Cabet, Étienne] (*pseud.* Francis Adams), 1788–1856.
      *Voyage et Aventures de Lord William Carisdall en Icarie,
      Traduits de l'Anglais de Francis Adams, Par Th. Dufruit.* 2
      vols. Paris, 1840. (Not written in English.)

      BN CSmH CtY ICN MH NN

175   ————.
      Voyage en Icarie. [With preface by the author.] Paris, 1842.
      566 p.

      BM BN CSmH CtY ICN   1845: NN   1846: DLC
      1848: ICU MH NcD

      [A summary in English by J. Max Patrick appears in *The
      Quest for Utopia,* by Glenn Negley and J. Max Patrick, chap.
      31 (New York, 1952, 1962, 1971).]

176   ————.
      *Colonie Icarienne aux États-Unis d'Amérique. Sa constitution,
      ses lois, sa situation matérielle et morale, après le premier
      semestre 1855.* Paris, 1856. 240 p.

      BN CSmH CtY DLC ICN ICU MH NcD NN

177   Cadei, Luigi.
      Dalla Terra Alla 7. Molecola. Milan, 1949. 82 p.

      DLC NN

178   Cadmus and Harmonia (*pseuds.*). *See* Buchan, John and Susan.

179   [Callenbach, Franz] (*pseud.* Vermelio Wurmsaam), 1663–1743.
      *Wurmland nach Lands-Art, Regiment, Religion, Sitten und
      Lebens-Wandel . . . Bey Vermelio Wurmsaam; Im Gast-Haus
      zum Regenwurm. Im Jahr da Es Wurmstichig War.* Nurem-
      berg, 1710(?). 128 p.

      BM CtY ICU   1715: ICN

180   *Il Calzolaio e le Scarpe, Ossia l'Isola Pacifica.* N.p. (Italy), n.d. (Probably late 18th c.) 39 p.

NcD

181   Campanella, Tommaso, 1568–1639.
Politicae Civitas Solis Idea Reipublicae Philosophicae. Appendix to Part 4 of *Realis Philosophiae Epilogisticae.* Frankfurt, 1623. (Probably written 1602–3.)

BM BN ICU MH NcD NN   1643: CSmH CtY
1836: DLC   1854: ICN

[The most authoritative recent edition is *La Città del Sole,* edited by Norberto Bobbio (Turin, 1941). The only satisfactory English translation is that of William J. Gilstrap in *The Quest for Utopia,* by Glenn Negley and J. Max Patrick, chap. 19 (New York, 1952, 1962, 1971).]

182   Capek, Karel, 1890–1938.
R. U. R. (Rossum's Universal Robots). Translated by Paul Selver. New York, 1922. 187 p.

MH NN   1923: BM CtY DLC ICN ICU NcD
1924 (French): BN

183   Capon, Paul, 1912–.
The Other Side of the Sun. London, 1950. 321 p.

BM DLC MH NcD NN

184   ————.
Into the Tenth Millenium. London, 1956. 275 p.

BM

185   [Carrel, Frederic.]
2010. London, 1914. 249 p.

BM NN

186   [Caryl, Charles W.]
New Era. Denver, 1897. 192 p.

CSmH CtY DLC ICN ICU MH NcD NN

187   Casanova de Seingalt, Giacomo Girolamo, 1725–1798.
       *Icosameron; ou, Histoire d'Édouard et d'Élisabeth Qui Passèrent
       Quatre Vingte Un Ans chez les Mégamicres Habitans Abori-
       gènes du Protocosme dans l'Intérieur de Notre Globe, Traduite
       de l'Anglois* ... 5 vols. Prague, 1787.

       BM NN   1788: CtY DLC ICN MH

188   Cassola, Gaspare Luigi, 1745–1809.
       Poema sopra la Pluralità dei Mondi. Milan, 1774. 132 p.

       ICN NcD

189   Catelani, Arturo, 1860–.
       Nel Mondo del Possible; l'Italia nel 19 ... *Lettere alla "Gazetta
       del Belucistan."* Rome, 1926. 189 p.

       NN

190   Cavendish, Margaret, duchess of Newcastle. *See* Newcastle.

191   Centennius, Ralph (*pseud.*).
       The Dominion in 1983. Peterborough, Ontario, 1883. 30 p.

       BM NN

192   Chambless, Edgar.
       Roadtown. New York, 1910. 172 p.

       BM CSmH CtY DLC MH NN

193   Chappuys, Gabriel, 1546–1611.
       "De la République d'Utopie, Éstat et Gouvernement d'Icelle."
       In *L'Éstat, Description et Gouvernement des Royaumes et Ré-
       publiques du Monde, Tant Anciennes que Modernes,* book 24.
       Paris, 1585.

       BN CtY DLC   1598: BM Bod ICN

194   Chateau, Henri, 1870–.
       La Cité des Idoles. Roman inédit. Paris, 1906. 283 p.

       BN NcD

195 Chavannes, Albert, 1836–1903.
The Future Commonwealth or, What Samuel Balcom Saw in Socioland. New York, 1892. 114 p. (First published in *The True Nationalist*, 1891.)

DLC ICN MH NcD NN   1895: CSmH

196 ————.
In Brighter Climes, or Life in Socioland. Knoxville, Tenn., 1895. 254 p.

CSmH ICN   1897: DLC ICU NN

197 Chester, Lord (*pseud.*). *See* Teed, Cyrus Romulus Reed.

198 Chesterton, Gilbert Keith, 1874–1936.
The Return of Don Quixote. London, 1927. 311 p.

BM CSmH CtY DLC ICN ICU MH NcD NN
1928 (French): BN

199 [Chetwood, William Rufus] (*pseud.* Capt. Robert Boyle), *d.* 1766.
The Voyages and Adventures of Captain Robert Boyle, in Several Parts of the World. London, 1726. 374 p.

BM CSmH CtY DLC ICN MH NN   1730 (French): BN
1735: NcD   1796: ICU

200 Chiari, Pietro, 1711–1785.
L'Uomo d'un Altro Mondo o Sia Memorie d'un Solitario Senze Nome, Scritte da Lui Medesimo in Due Linguaggi, Chinese, e Russiano, e Pubblicate nella Nostra Lingue dall' Abbate Pietro Chiari. Venice, 1768.

MH

201 ————.
L'Isole della Fortuna; o sia, Viaggi de Missi Jalingh, Scritti da lei Medesima. 4 vols. Naples, 1774.

1776: BM NcD   1787: CtY

202 Chilton, Henry Herman.
The Lost Children. London, 1931. 288 p.

BM

203   Chirac, Auguste, 1838–.
      Si. Étude Sociale d'Après-Demain. Paris, 1893. 334 p.
      BN CtY NcD

204   Cignano, Lodovico.
      Quieta Solitudine di Varii Ragionamenti . . . Discorsi et Con-
      cetti, Ove si Narra Quattro Navigationi Fatte d'Alcuni Mer-
      canti, & delle Lor Merci & di sua Fortuna, Paesi & Popoli da
      Lor Vedati. Bologna, 1587. 166 p.
      BM ICN NcD

205   Cirkel, August.
      Looking Forward. Chicago, 1906. 365 p.
      DLC ICN NcD NN

206   Clapperton, Jane Hume.
      A Vision of the Future, Based on the Application of Ethical
      Principles. London, 1904. 347 p.
      BM BN DLC NN

207   Clarke, F. H. (*pseud.* Zebina Forbush).
      The Co-opolitan. Chicago, 1898. 170 p.
      1975: DLC NcD NN

208   [Clemens, Samuel Langhorne] (*pseud.* Mark Twain), 1835–1910.
      The Curious Republic of Gondour. New York, 1919. 140 p.
      (Published in *Galaxy,* May 1870–April 1871.)
      CSmH ICN ICU DLC MH NcD   Works: CtY

209   [————].
      Extract from Capt. Stormfield's Visit to Heaven. New York,
      1909. 120 p. (Published in *Harpers,* December 1907–January
      1908.)
      BM CSmH CtY DLC ICN ICU MH NcD NN

210   Clément, Augustin Jean Charles, bishop, 1717–1804.
      Mémoire sur la Partie du Globe della Terre Qui a Été Long-
      tems Découverte, et Habitée sous le Nom de l'Atlantide, et
      depuis Disparue sous les Eaux. Paris, 1803. 29 p.
      NcD

211 Clough, Fred M.
  The Golden Age; or, the Depth of Time. Boston, 1923. 192 p.
  DLC NN

212 Clowes, Sir William Laird, 1856–1905.
  The Captain of the "Mary Rose"; a Tale of Tomorrow. London, 1892. 308 p.
  BM NcD

213 ————.
  The Double Emperor. A Story of a Vagabond Cunarder. London, 1894. 238 p.
  BM NcD

214 Clyde, Irene.
  Beatrice the Sixteenth. London, 1909. 338 p.
  BM

215 [Cobbe, Frances Power] (*pseud.* Merlin Nostradamus), 1882–1904.
  The Age of Science: a Newspaper of the 20th Century. London, 1877. 50 p.
  BM CtY MH NcD NN

216 Coblentz, Stanton Arthur, 1896–.
  The Sunken World. Los Angeles, 1948. 184 p.
  CSmH CtY DLC NcD 1950: ICN 1951: BM

217 *Codicilles de Louys XIII, Roy de France et de Navarre, à Son Très Cher Fils Aisné Successeur*. Paris (?), 1643.
  BM BN CtY MH 1720: ICN

218 ————.
  Un Utopiste Inconnu. Les "Codicilles" de Louis XIII. Edited by Georges Lacour-Gayet. Paris, 1903. 51 p.
  BM BN ICN NN

219 Colburn, Frona Eunice Wait (Smith), 1859–.
  Yermah the Dorado; the Story of a Lost Race. San Francisco, 1897. 350 p.
  BM DLC MH 1913: CSmH NcD NN

220   Cole, Cyrus.
        The Aurora Phone; a Romance. Chicago, 1890. 249 p.

        BM CSmH DLC ICU NcD NN

221   Cole, Robert William.
        The Struggle for Empire. A Story of the Year 2236. London, 1900. 213 p.

        BM

222   Cooke, Donald Ewin, 1916–.
        The History of Lewistonia. Point Highest (Chicago?), 1934. 219 p.

        NcD

223   [Cooper, J. C.]
        The Handwriting on the Wall; or, Revolution in 1907. St. Louis, 1903. 377 p.

        CSmH DLC ICU MH NcD

224   [Cooper, James Fenimore], 1789–1851.
        The Crater; or, Vulcan's Peak. 2 vols. New York, 1847. (*Mark's Reef; or, the Crater.* 3 vols. London, 1847.)

        BM BN CSmH CtY DLC ICN MH NN   1854: NcD
        1885: ICU

225   Corbett, Elizabeth Burgoyne.
        New Amazonia: a Foretaste of the Future. London, 1889. 146 p.

        BM

226   Corvo, Baron Frederick (*pseud.*). *See* Rolfe, Frederick William.

227   [Cory, Vivian] (*pseud.* Victoria Cross).
        Martha Brown, M.P. A Girl of To-morrow. London, 1935. 256 p.

        BM NcD

228   [Coste, Frank Hill Perry (Perrycoste)] (*pseud.* A Free Lance). *Towards Utopia (Being Speculations in Social Evolution).* London and New York, 1894. 252 p.

     BM CtY DLC ICN ICU MH NcD NN

229   Cousin-Jacques (*pseud.*). *See* Beffroy de Reigny, Louis Abel.

230   Coutan (maître-boutonnier). *Le Livre Sans Titre, à l'Usage de Ceux Qui Sont Éveilles pour les Endormir; et de Ceux Qui Sont Endormis, pour les Éveiller.* Amsterdam and Paris, 1775. 204 p.

     BN DLC   1778: NcD

231   Coverdale, Sir Henry Standish (*pseud.*). *The Fall of the Great Republic.* Boston, 1885. 226 p.

     BM CSmH DLC ICU NcD NN

232   Cowan, James, 1841–. *Daybreak; a Romance of an Old World.* New York, 1896. 399 p.

     BM CSmH CtY DLC NcD NN

233   Coyer, l'abbé Gabriel François, 1707–1782. *A Discovery of the Island Frivola . . . Wrote by Order of A——l A——n.* London, 1750. 40 p.

     CtY MH

234   ————. *Découverte de l'Îsle Frivole.* The Hague, 1751. 52 p.

     BN

235   ————. *A Supplement to Lord Anson's Voyage Around the World, Containing a Discovery and Description of the Island of Frivola.* London, 1752. 63 p.

     BM CSmH DLC ICN NN

236 ————.

    Chinki; Histoire Cochinchinoise, Qui Peut Servir à d'Autres Pays. London, 1768. 96 p.

    BM BN CtY DLC ICN ICU NcD NN

237 Craig, Alexander.
    Ionia; Land of Wise Men and Fair Women. Chicago, 1898. 301 p.

    BM DLC NN

238 Cram, Ralph Adams, 1863–1942.
    Walled Towns. Boston, 1919. 105 p.

    CtY DLC ICU NcD NN   1920: BM MH

239 Cranmer-Byng, Launcelot Alfred, 1872–.
    Tomorrow's Star, an Essay on the Shattering and Remoulding of a World. London, 1928. 179 p.

    BM DLC NN

240 Cridge, Alfred Denton.
    Utopia; or the History of an Extinct Planet. Oakland, Calif., 1884. 30 p.

    DLC NcD

241 [Crocker, Samuel] (*pseud.* Theodore Oceanic Islet), 1845–1921.
    That Island. Kansas City, Mo., 1892. 156 p.

    DLC NN

242 Croft-Cooke, Rupert, 1903–.
    Cosmopolis. London, 1932. 331 p.

    BM DLC   1933: NcD NN   1937: BN

243 Croly, David Goodman, 1829–1889.
    Glimpses of the Future; Suggestions as to the Drift of Things . . . (To Be Read Now and Judged in the Year 2000). New York, 1888. 177 p.

    ICU NcD NN

244   [Croly, Herbert David] (*pseud.* William Herbert), 1869–1930.
The World Grown Young. Being a Brief Record of Reforms Carried out from 1894–1914 by the Late Mr. P. Adams, Millionaire and Philanthropist. London, 1892. 304 p.

BM

245   Cross, Victoria (*pseud.*). *See* Cory, Vivian.

246   Crotti, Carlo.
Progretto di una Nuova Capitale di Vasto Regno. Cremona, 1844.

NN

247   Cyrano de Bergerac, Savinien, 1619–1655.
Histoire Comique des États et Empires de la Lune. Paris, 1657. 191 p.

BN MH   1659: DLC ICN   1676: NcD   1858: BM
1875: ICU

248   ————.
L'histoire des États et Empires du Soleil. (In Cyrano's *Nouvelles Oeuvres.*) Paris, 1662.

BN ICN   1676: NcD   1858: BM DLC   1875: ICU

249   ————.
Voyages to the Moon and the Sun. Translated by Richard Aldington. London and New York, 1923, 1962. 329 p.

BM CSmH CtY DLC ICN ICU MH NcD

250   D***
Les Chaines Brisées, ou le Retour à la Nature. 2 vols. in 1. Paris, 1803.

BN NcD

251   D., C. ***. *See* Rustaing de Saint-Jory, Louis.

252   Dague, Robert Addison, 1841–.
Henry Ashton: a Thrilling Story and How the Famous Co-

operative Commonwealth Was Established in Zanland. Alameda, Calif. 1903. 235 p.

CSmH CtY DLC MH NcD NN

253 Daneau, Lambert, 1530–*ca.* 1595.
Politices Christianae. Geneva, 1595. 576 p.
BM

254 Daniel, Charles S.
Ai. A Social Vision. Philadelphia, 1892. 296 p.
BM CSmH CtY DLC NcD

255 [Daniel, Gabriel], 1649–1728.
Voyage du Monde de Descartes. Paris, 1690. 437 p.
BN CtY DLC ICU MH   1691: BM   1739: NcD

256 [————].
A Voyage to the World of Cartesius. Translated by T. Taylor.
London, 1692. 298 p.
BM CSmH CtY ICN MH   1694: DLC ICU NcD

257 D'Arusmont, Frances Wright. *See* Wright, Frances.

258 Daudet, Léon, 1867–1942.
Le Napus, Fléau de l'An 2227. Paris, 1927. 309 p.
BN DLC

259 D'Avenant, Sir William, 1606–1668.
A Discourse upon Gondibert. Paris, 1650; London, 1651. 145 p.
BM BN CSmH CtY MH NN   1651: DLC ICN
ICU NcD

260 Davenport, Basil, 1905–.
An Introduction to Islandia, Its History, Customs, Laws, Language, and Geography . . . History and Description by Jean Perrier, First French Consul to Islandia; and Translated by John Lang, First American Consul. New York, 1942. 61 p.
(*See* Wright, Austin Tappan.)
CtY DLC MH NcD NN   1951: BM

261 [Davis, Ellis James.]
   Pyrna, a Commune; or, Under the Ice. London, 1875. 142 p.
   BM

262 [————.]
   Coralia, a Plaint of Futurity. London, 1876. 217 p.
   BM

263 Davis, Nathan.
   Beulah; or, a Parable of Social Regeneration. Kansas City, Mo.,
   1904. 301 p.
   DLC ICN MH

264 *The Dawn of the Twentieth Century. A Novel, Social and Political.*
   3 vols. London, 1882.
   BM   1898: DLC

265 Dazergues, Max André.
   L'Île Aerienne. Paris, 1946. 239 p.
   BN

266 Dearmer, Geoffrey, 1893-.
   Saint on Holiday. London, 1933. 337 p.
   BM NcD

267 [De Bury, Mme. F. Blaze] (*pseud.* F. Dickberry).
   The Storm of London. A Social Rhapsody. London, 1904.
   313 p.
   BM ICN NcD   1905: DLC

268 [Defoe, Daniel], 1661-1731.
   *The Consolidator; or, Memoirs of Sundry Transactions from
   the World in the Moon, Translated from the Lunar Language.*
   London, 1705. 360 p.
   BM CSmH CtY DLC ICN ICU MH NcD NN

269 de Graffigny, Henri. *See* Le Faure, Georges.

270 De Grave. *See* Graves, Charles Joseph de.

271 Delbrück, Georges.
    Au Pays de l'Harmonie: Beauté, Harmonie, Amour. Paris, 1906. 312 p.

    BN NcD

272 [DeMille, James] (*pseud.* Gilbert Gaul), 1837–1880.
    A Strange Manuscript Found in a Copper Cylinder. New York, 1888. 291 p.

    BM CSmH CtY DLC ICU MH NcD   1894: NN

273 Democritus, Junior (*pseud.*). *See* Burton, Robert.

274 [Denison, Thomas Stewart], 1848–1911.
    An Iron Crown. A Tale of the Great Republic. Chicago, 1885. 560 p.

    CSmH DLC ICN ICU NcD NN

275 [Desfontaines, Pierre François Guyot] (L. D. F.), 1685–1745.
    Le Nouveau Gulliver, ou Voyage de Jean Gulliver, Fils du Capitaine Gulliver, Traduit d'un Manuscrit Anglois, par Monsieur L. D. F. 2 vols. Paris and Amsterdam, 1730.

    BM BN CtY DLC ICN ICU MH NcD NN
    1787: CSmH

276 [————].
    The Travels of Mr. John Gulliver, Son to Capt. Lemuel Gulliver. Translated by J. Lockman. 2 vols. London, 1731.

    BM CtY ICN NN

277 Desmond, Shaw, 1877–.
    Ragnarok. London, 1926. 351 p.

    BM NcD

278 Detre, L.
    Kampf Zweiter Welten. Vienna, 1935. 278 p.

    DLC

279 ——————.
> *War of Two Worlds.* London, 1936. 253 p.
> BM MH

280 Devinne, Paul.
> *The Day of Prosperity. A Vision of the Century to Come.* New York, 1902. 271 p.
> BM DLC NcD

281 Dick, Mr. (*pseud.*).
> *James Ingleton: The History of a Social State. A.D. 2000.* London, 1887. 450 p.
> BM NcD

282 Dickberry, F. (*pseud.*). *See* DeBury, Mme. F. Blaze.

283 Dietsch, Andreas.
> *Das Tausendjährige Reich, Nebst Plan und Statuten zer Gründung von New-Helvetia im staate Missouri in Nord-Amerika.* Aarau (?), 1844 (?). 95 p.
> DLC   1854: NN

284 Dioscorides, Dr. (*pseud.*). *See* Harting, Pieter.

285 Diplomat, A. (*pseud.*).
> *Rise and Fall of the United States; a Leaf from History, A.D. 2060.* New York, 1898.
> ICN

286 Disraeli, Benjamin. *See* Beaconsfield.

287 Dixie, Lady Florence Caroline (Douglas), 1857–1905.
> *Gloriana, or, the Revolution of 1900.* London, 1890. 350 p.
> BM

288 Dixon, Thomas, Jr., 1864–1946.
> *Comrades; a Story of Social Adventure in California.* New York, 1909. 319 p.
> BM CtY DLC MH NcD NN

289 Dodd, Mrs. Anna Bowman (Blake), 1855–1929.
The Republic of the Future; or, Socialism a Reality. New York, 1887. 86 p.

CtY DLC ICN ICU MH NcD NN

290 Dominik, Hans Joachim, 1872–1946.
Die Macht der Drei; ein Roman aus dem Jahre 1955. Leipzig, 1922. 359 p.

DLC   1943: CtY ICU MH NN

291 Doni, Antonio Francesco, 1513–1574.
I Mondi ... Libro Primo. Venice, 1552. 120 ff.

BM BN Bod DLC MH

292 ————.

Inferni, Libro Secondo de Mondi. Venice, 1553. 224 p.

Bod CtY ICN MH   1597: DLC

293 ————.

Mondi Celesti, Terrestri, et Infernali, de Gli Accademici Pellegrini. Venice, 1562. 430 p.

BM NcD NN   1567: ICN   1568: BN MH
1575: CtY   1583: DLC   1606: ICU

294 [Donnelly, Ignatius] (*pseud.* Edmund Boisgilbert, M.D.), 1831–1901.
Caesar's Column. A Story of the Twentieth Century. New York, 1890. 367 p.

BM CSmH CtY DLC ICN MH NcD NN   19——: ICU

295 [————].
Caesar's Column. . . . Edited by Walter B. Rideout. Cambridge, Mass., 1960.

BM BN CtY DLC ICU MH NcD NN

296 Dooner, Pierton W., 1844–1907.
The Last Days of the Republic. San Francisco, 1880. 258 p.

BN CSmH CtY DLC MH NcD NN

297   Dopico Otero, Manuel.
       Antorcha Universal del Porvenir. La Coruña, 1935.

       MH

298   Dossi, Carlo, 1849–1910.
       La Colonia Felice. Milan, 1874. 170 p.

       BM DLC NN   1910: ICU   Works: BN

299   Dougall, Lily, 1858–1923.
       The Christ That Is to Be. New York, 1907. 385 p. (Published
       in Great Britain as *Christus Futurus.*)

       Bod CtY DLC ICU NN

300   [Douglass, Ellsworth.]
       *Pharoah's Broker: Being the Very Remarkable Experiences in
       Another World of Isidore Werner.* London, 1899. 316 p.

       BM NcD

301   Dovski, Lee van (*pseud.*). *See* Lewandowski, Herbert.

302   Drane, Augusta Theodosia (Mother Frances Raphael, O.S.D.),
       1823–1894.
       The New Utopia. London, 1898. 184 p.

       BM

303   Duchesne, Etiénne Julien François.
       *Proposition de Former une République Suivant le Plan du
       Président de Montesquieu, dans les Montagnes de la Guyane
       Française.* Blois, 1802. 48 p.

       BN CtY MH

304   [Dudgeon, Robert Ellis], 1820–1904.
       Colymbia. London, 1873. 255 p.

       BM MH

305   Du Maurier, George Louis Palmella Busson, 1834–1896.
       The Martian; a Novel. London and New York, 1897. 477 p.

       BM BN CSmH CtY DLC ICN ICU MH NcD NN

306   [Duperron de Castera, Louis Adrien], 1705–1752.
       *Le Théâtre des Passions et de la Fortune, ou les Aventures Sur-
       prenantes de Rosamidor & de Théoglaphire. Histoire Australe.*
       Paris, 1731. 352 p.

       BM BN ICN MH

307   Du Quesne, Henri, marquis.
       *Un projet de République à l'Île d'Éden . . . Réimpression d'un
       Ouvrage Disparu, Publié en 1689.* Edited by Th. Sauzier. Paris,
       1887. 120 p.

       BM BN CtY ICN ICU MH

308   Edson, Milan C.
       Solaris Farm, A Story of the Twentieth Century. Washington,
       D.C., 1900. 447 p.

       CSmH CtY DLC ICU NN

309   Ehrhardt, Paul Georg, 1889–.
       Die Letzte Macht, eine Utopie aus Unserer Zeit; Roman. Mu-
       nich, 1921. 240 p.

       CtY DLC MH

310   *Eliana, A New Romance Formed by an English Hand.* London,
       1661. 289 p.

       BM CtY ICN MH

311   Eliot, John, 1604–1690.
       *The Christian Commonwealth: or the Civil Policy of the Rising
       Kingdom of Jesus Christ. Written Before the Interruption of
       the Government.* London, 1659. 84 p.

       BM CSmH CtY DLC NN

312   —————.
       The Christian Commonwealth. . . . Collections of Massachu-
       setts Historical Society, no. 34. Boston, 1937.

       CtY DLC ICN NcD

313 Ellis, G. A.
New Britain. A Narrative of a Journey by Mr. Ellis, to a Country So Called by Its Inhabitants, Discovered in the Vast Plain of the Missouri, in North America, and Inhabited by a People of British Origin. London, 1820. 336 p.

CSmH CtY DLC ICN ICU MH NcD NN

314 Ellis, Henry Havelock, 1859–1939.
The Nineteenth Century. A Dialogue in Utopia. London, 1900. 166 p.

BM CSmH CtY DLC ICU MH NN

315 [Emanuel, Victor Rousseau] (*pseud*. Victor Rousseau), 1879–.
The Messiah of the Cylinder. Chicago and London, 1917. 319 p.

BM DLC MH NcD NN

316 Emanuel, Walter, 1869–1915.
One Hundred Years Hence. Being Some Extracts from "The Hourly Mail." London, 1911. 76 p.

BM NN

317 Emerson, Willis George, 1856–.
The Smoky God. Chicago, 1908. 186 p.

BM DLC NcD

318 *The Emigrants: or, the Island of Esmeralda. By the author of "Atlantis."* N.p., 1879. 64 p.

DLC NcD

319 *Equality; or, a History of Lithconia.* Philadelphia, 1837. [Published 1802 in *The Temple of Reason*, deist newspaper, Philadelphia; author may have been Dr. James Reynolds.]

CSmH

320 *Equality. . . .* Edited by A. C. P. Philadelphia, 1947. 86 p.

CSmH CtY DLC ICN ICU NcD NN

40

321 Ernst, Morris Leopold, 1888–.
     Utopia, 1976. New York, 1955. 305 p.

     BM CtY DLC ICN ICU MH NcD NN

322 Erskine, Thomas Erskine, baron, 1750–1823.
     Armata: A Fragment. London, 1817. 210 p.

     BM CtY DLC ICN MH NcD NN

323 ———.
     The Second Part of Armata. London, 1817. 209 p.

     BM CtY

324 [E. R. V. F. L.]
     Relation du Voyage de l'Îsle d'Eutopie. Delft, 1711; Paris, 1716.
     240 p.

     MH NcD   1716: ICN

325 Espinosa, Juan, 1804–1871.
     Mi Republica . . . Justicia y Verdad. New York, 1854. 53 p.

     BM CtY NN

326 *An Essay Concerning Adepts . . . With Some Resolution Concern-*
     ing the Principles of the Adeptists; and a Model, Practicable,
     and Easy, of Living in Community. In Two Parts. By a Phila-
     dept. London, 1698. 52 p.

     BM ICN

327 *Etymonia.* London, 1875. 258 p.

     BM

328 Evans, Chris, *d.* 1924.
     Eurasia. San Francisco, 1900. 82 p.

     NN

329 Evans, Idrisyn Oliver, 1894–.
     The World of To-Morrow. London, 1933. 163 p.

     BM DLC

330   [Eveille, Garson.]
       Trompgarso on the Back of the Moon. Philadelphia, 1832.
       12 p.

       NN

331   Even, James Eugene, 1900–.
       Another World. Boston, 1954. 124 p.

       DLC NcD NN

332   F., L. D. *See* Desfontaines, Pierre François Guyot.

333   Falkiner, Caesar Litton, 1863–1908.
       "Address Delivered in the Dining Hall of Trinity College . . .
       on Thursday Evening, November 5th, 1885." At head of title:
       The New Voyage to Utopia. Dublin, 1885. 74 p.

       BM DLC

334   Faramond, Ludwig Ernst von (*pseud.*). *See* Sinold, Philipp Bal-
       thasar.

335   Farnell, George.
       Rev. Josiah Hilton, the Apostle of the New Age. Providence,
       R.I., 1898. 94 p.

       CtY DLC

336   Farningham, Marianne (*pseud.*). *See* Hearn, Mary Ann.

337   Faure, Sébastien, 1857/8–1942.
       Mon Opinion sur la Dictature. Paris, 1921. 46 p.

       NcD

338   [Fawkes, Frank Attfield] (*pseud.* X).
       *Marmaduke, Emperor of Europe. Being a Record of Some
       Strange Adventures in the Remarkable Career of a Political and
       Social Reformer Who Was Famous at the Commencement of
       the Twentieth Century.* Chelmsford and London, 1895. 271 p.

       BM CSmH NcD

339   Fayard, Marcello I.
Hacia la Edad de Oro. Buenos Aires, 19–.
NN

340   Fedeli, Ugo.
Un Viaggio alle "Isole Utopia," Conversazioni Tenute in Ivrea al "Centro Culturale Olivetti" (Gennaio-Febbraio, 1958). Ivrea (?), 1958. 200 p.
DLC

341   Fénelon, François de Salignac de la Mothe, 1651–1715.
Suite du Quatrième Livre de l'Odysée d'Homère, ou les Avantures de Télémaque, Fils d'Ulysse. Paris, 1699. 208 p.

BM BN CtY ICN MH   1701: NcD   1717: NN
1720: DLC   1730: ICU   1732: CSmH

[The 700-odd entries in 14 languages under this title in the Catalogue Générale of the Bibliothéque Nationale for 1929 are by no means an exhaustive listing. The earliest English translations are given below, as well as one of the most available translations in English.]

342   ————.
Adventures of Telemachus. Translated [by I. Littlebury]. Part 1. London, 1699. 152 p.
BM

343   ————.
Adventures of Telemachus the Son of Ulysses. In Five Parts. Translated [by I. Littlebury]. 2 vols. London, 1701.
BM

344   ————.
The Adventures of Telemachus, the Son of Ulysses. Translated by T. Smollett. 2 vols. London, 1776.
BM CSmH CtY ICN ICU MH NcD   1786: NN

345   Fenn, Louis Anderson.
The Project of a Planned World. London, 1933. 72 p.
BM DLC ICU NN

346   *A Few Things Worth Knowing About the Heretofore Unexplored Country of Theopolis.* London, 1853. 78 p.

CtY

347   Fialko, Nathan, 1881–.
The New City. Translated by the author. New York, 1937. 153 p.

BM BN CtY DLC ICN ICU MH NcD

348   Fieux. *See* Mouhy, Charles de Fieux, chevalier de.

349   Finlay, James Colin.
Time Shall Be Neutral. Auckland, 1963. 63 p.

NcD

350   Finney, Charles Grandison, 1905–.
The Unholy City. New York, 1937. 167 p.

CtY DLC MH NcD NN

351   Firmiano, Petro. *See* Zacharie de Lisieux.

352   Flecker, James Elroy, 1884–1915.
The Last Generation. A Story of the Future. London, 1908. 56 p.

BM CSmH CtY ICN ICU MH NcD NN

353   Fleury, Claude, 1640–1723.
Les Moeurs des Israëlites, òu l'On Voit le Modèle d'une Politique Simple & Sincère pour le Gouvernement des États & la Réforme des Moeurs. Paris and The Hague, 1681. 348 p.

BN NN   1682: DLC   1683: BM   1701: ICU
1732: CtY   1763: ICN NcD   1771: MH

354   ————.

Manners of the Ancient Israelites: Containing an Account of Their Peculiar Customs and Ceremonies, Their Laws, Polity, Religion, Sects, Arts and Trades. Translated by Adam Clarke. London, 1802; Burlington, Vt., 1813; New York, 1837. 386 p.

BM CSmH CtY DLC ICU MH NcD NN

355 ————.

> *A Short History of the Ancient Israelites.* Baltimore, 1811.
> 307 p.

> MH NcD NN

356 Flower, Benjamin Orange, 1858–1918.

> *Equality and Brotherhood, the Dreams of the Ancient World,*
> *Become Realities of To-day* . . . *With Particular Reference to*
> *Edward Bellamy's Work on "Equality" and the Verification of*
> *That Work in the Existing Conditions of Civilization.* Boston,
> 1897. 19 p.

> DLC

357 Floyd, Thomas, *fl.* 1603.

> *The Picture of a Perfit Common Wealth, Describing As Well*
> *the Offices of Princes and Inferiour Magistrates Over Their*
> *Subjects, as Also the Duties of Subjects Towards Their Gover-*
> *nours. Gathered Forth of Many Authors, Aswel Humane, as*
> *Divine.* London, 1600. 309 p.

> BM CSmH

358 Flürscheim, Michael, 1844–1912.

> *Deutschland in Hundert Jahren, oder die Galoschen des Glücks.*
> Dresden and Leipzig, 1890. 85 p.

> CtY DLC MH   1891: BM

359 Foigny, Gabriel de (*pseud.* Jacques Sadeur), ca. 1650–1692.

> *La Terre Australe Connue, C'est à Dire, la Description de ce*
> *Pays Inconnu Jusqu'Ici, de Ses Moeurs et de Ses Coûtumes,*
> *par M. Sadeur.* Vannes (i.e., Geneva), 1676. 267 p.

> BM BN ICN NN   1692: CtY DLC MH NcD
> 1788: CSmH

360 ————.

> *La Terre Australe Connue. . . .* In *Les Successeurs de Cyrano*
> *de Bergerac,* by Frédéric Lachèvre, pp. 1–166. Paris, 1922.

> BM BN CtY DLC ICN ICU MH NcD NN

361 ————.

A New Discovery of Terra Incognita Australis, or the Southern World . . . by James Sadeur, a French-man. London, 1693. 186 p.

BM DLC ICN MH NN

362 Folingsby, Kenneth.
Meda: a Tale of the Future. Glasgow, 1891. 325 p.

BM ICN NcD   1892: CtY

363 Follin, Henri Léon, 1886–.
La Révolution du 4 Septembre, 19–. Paris, 1921. 259 p.

BN NN

364 ————.

La Métapolitique Supra Nationale; Genese et Evolution de Son Concept et d'un Organisation Adequate. Paris, 1927. 38 p.

BN NN

365 Fontaines, Louis. See Zacherie de Lisieux.

366 [Fontenelle, Bernard le Bovier de], 1657–1757 (probable author).
Entretiens sur la Pluralité des Mondes. Paris, 1686. 359 p.

BM BN   1687: CtY   1694: NN   1701: CSmH NcD
1707: MH   1719: ICU   1784: ICN   1821: DLC

367 [————].
Entretiens sur la Pluralité des Mondes. Edited by R. Shackleton. London, 1955. 219 p.

BN Bod CtY DLC ICN ICU MH NcD NN

368 [————].
A Plurality of Worlds. Translated by John Glanvill. London, 1688. 152 p.

BM CtY ICN MH   1702: NcD   1719: ICU
1728: BN

369 [————].
A Plurality of Worlds. Translated by John Glanvill. Edited by David Garnett. London, 1929. 188 p.

BM CSmH CtY DLC ICN ICU MH NN

370 [————].
A Discovery of New Worlds. Translated by Aphra Behn. London, 1688. 158 p.

BM CSmH CtY DLC ICU NN   1718: ICN
1737: NcD

371 [————].
Conversations on the Plurality of Worlds. Translated by W. Gardiner. London, 1715. 192 p.

BM BN DLC ICN ICU MH NcD   1728: CSmH

372 [————].
Conversations on the Plurality of Worlds. Dublin, 1761. 226 p.

CSmH ICN NcD

373 [————].
La République des Philosophes, ou, Histoire des Ajaoiens, Ouvrage Posthume de Mr. de Fontenelle. Geneva, 1768. 188 p.

BM BN MH

374 Forbush, Zebina (pseud.). See Clarke, F. H.

375 [Ford, Douglas Morey.]
The Raid of Dover: a Romance of the Reign of Woman, A.D. 1940. London, 1910. 188 p.

BM NcD

376 Formaleoni, Vincenzio Antonio, 1752–1797.
Caterin Zeno. Storia Curiosa delle Sue Avventure in Persia, Tratta da un Antico Originale Manoscritto, ed Ora per la Prima Volta Pubblicata da V. Formaleoni. Venice, 1783. 118 p.

BM NcD

47

377   Forrest, Henry J.
         A Dream of Reform. London, 1848.

         BM

378   Forster, Edward Morgan, 1879–.
         "The Machine Stops." In *The Eternal Moment and Other Stories,* chap. 1. London, 1928.

         BM CSmH CtY DLC ICN ICU MH NcD NN

379   Fougeret de Monbron, Louis Charles, *ca.* 1720–1761.
         Le Cosmopolite, ou le Citoyen du Monde. London (Amsterdam?), 1753. 165 p.

         BM BN CtY NcD   1761: DLC

380   Fowler, George.
         A Flight to the Moon; or, the Vision of Randalthus. Baltimore, 1813. 185 p.

         CSmH CtY DLC ICN MH NN

381   Fowler, Sydney (*pseud.*). *See* Wright, Sydney Fowler.

382   Fox, Lady Mary, ed. (Sometimes attributed to Richard Whately.)
         Account of an Expedition (Planned and Conducted by Mr. H. Sibthorpe) to the Interior of New Holland. London, 1837. 243 p.

         BM BN CtY DLC ICN MH NcD NN

383   ————.
         The Southlanders, an Account of an Expedition to the Interior of New Holland. London, 1849.

         BM

384   [Fox, Samuel Middleton], 1856–.
         Our Own Pompeii. A Romance of Tomorrow. 2 vols. Edinburgh, 1887.

         BM NcD

385   France, Anatole, 1844–1924.
       Sur la Pierre Blanche. Paris, 1903. 320 p.
       BM BN CtY DLC   1905: MH NN   19–: ICU
       n.d.: NcD

386   ———.
       The White Stone. Translated by C. E. Roche. London and
       New York, 1910. 239 p.
       DLC ICN ICU MH NcD NN   1926: CtY

387   ———.
       L'Île des Pingouins. Paris, 1908. 419 p.
       BM BN CtY DLC ICN ICU MH NN

388   ———.
       Penguin Island. Translated by A. W. Evans. London and
       New York, 1909. 345 p.
       BM CtY DLC ICN MH NN   1925: ICU NcD
       n.d.: BN

389   Francé, Raoul Heinrich, 1874–1943.
       *Phoebus: ein Rückblick auf das Glückliche Deutschland im
       Jahre 1980.* Munich, 1927. 81 p.

       DLC

390   Frank, Robert, 1893–.
       *Social Integration: a Brief Fictional History of the U.S. During
       the Period 1935–1945.* Boston, 1935. 199 p.

       CtY DLC ICU MH NcD NN

391   Frankau, Gilbert, 1884–1952.
       Unborn Tomorrow. London, 1953. 302 p.

       BM NcD

392   Franklin, Alfred Louis Auguste, 1830–1917.
       Les Ruines de Paris en 4875, Documents Officiels et Inédits.
       Paris, 1875. 92 p.

       BN Bod CtY NcD NN

393   A Free Lance (*pseud.*). *See* Coste, Frank Hill Perry.

394   Freeman, Nilekaw (*pseud.*). *See* Richardson, Jasper.

395   *The Free State of Noland.* London, 1696. 18 p. (Enlarged edition, London, 1701. 61 p.) [Sometimes catalogued *Noland.*]

     BM Bod CSmH ICN MH NcD

396   Friedliche, ———.
     Die Sociale Revolution am Anfange des Zwanzigsten Jahrhunderts; ein Zukunftsbild von einem Menschenfreunde. Munich, 1897. 87 p.

     BN NN

397   Frisbie, Henry Samuel.
     Prophet of the Kingdom. Washington, D.C., 1901. 238 p.

     DLC

398   Fuller, Lt. Alvarado Mortimer, 1851–.
     A.D. 2000. Chicago, 1890. 415 p.

     BM CSmH CtY DLC ICN NcD NN

399   Fuller, Frederick T.
     Beyond the Selvas; a Vision of a Republic That Might Have Been—and Still May Be. Boston, 1929. 95 p.

     MH NcD NN

400   Gale, Zona, 1874–1938.
     Romance Island. Indianapolis, 1906. 394 p.

     BM CtY DLC ICN ICU MH NcD NN

401   Gallet, Pierre.
     Voyage d'un Habitant de la Lune à Paris à la Fin du XVIIIe Siècle. Paris, 1803. 211 p.

     BN ICN NcD

402   [Galloway, James M.] (*pseud.* Anon Moore).
John Harvey; a Tale of the Twentieth Century. Chicago, 1897.
407 p. [Also published as *Lock and Key.*]

   DLC MH NcD NN

403   Galtié, Mathieu.
*Code Fondamental, ou Chartre du Genre Humain Déduite de
Ses Premiers Besoins.* Paris, 1830. 91 p.

   BN ICU

404   Gan "Index" (*pseud.*). *See* Williams, David Rhys.

405   Gancz, Fritz.
Der Weg der Wenigen. Vienna, 1953. 255 p.

   DLC MH NN

406   Gann, William D., 1878–.

The Tunnel Through the Air, or Looking Back from 1940.
New York, 1927. 418 p.

   DLC NcD

407   Ganpat (*pseud.*). *See* Gompertz, Martin Louis Alan.

408   [Garcilaso de la Vega (El Inca)], 1539–1616.
*Primera Parte de los Commentarios Reales, Que Tratan del
Origen de los Yncas.* Lisbon, 1609. 264 p.

   BM BN CSmH CtY DLC ICN MH NN

409   [————].
*Historia General del Perú Trata el Descubrimiento del; y Como
lo Ganaron los Españoles.* Cordoba, 1616. 300 p.

   BN DLC   1617: CSmH CtY ICN MH NN   1723: BM

410   [————].
Commentarios Reales. Edited by Giuseppe Bellini. Milan, 1955.
170 p.

   CtY MH NcD

411 [————].
The Incas; the Royal Commentaries of the Inca. Translated by
Maria Jolas. New York, 1961. 432 p.

BM CtY ICU MH NcD NN

412 [Gartmann, Heinz] (*pseud*. Werner Wehr), 1917–1960.
Ich Lebte im Jahr 3000; Roman einer Möglichen Reise. Stuttgart, 1959. 295 p.

DLC NcD NN

413 [Gaston, Henry A.]
Mars Revealed; or, Seven Days in the Spirit World. San Francisco, 1880. 208 p.

CSmH DLC NN

414 Gaul, Gilbert (*pseud*.). *See* DeMille, James.

415 Geissler, Ludwig A.
*Looking Beyond, a Sequel to "Looking Backward," by Edward
Bellamy, and an Answer to "Looking Further Forward," by
Richard Michaelis*. London, 1891. 102 p.

DLC NcD

416 Genone, Hudor (*pseud*.). *See* Roe, William James.

417 [Gentleman, Francis] (*pseud*. Sir Humphrey Lunatic, Bart.), 1728–
1784.
*A Trip to the Moon. Containing an Account of the Island of
Noibla. Its Inhabitants, Religious and Political Customs, &*.
2 vols. London, 1764–65.

BM CtY ICN

418 Gerhold, German (*pseud*.). *See* Schmidt, Willy.

419 Gerrare, Wirt (*pseud*.). *See* Greener, William Oliver.

420 *Geschiedkundige Beschryving van de Maan, Deszelfs Inwoonern en
zyn Beste Regeerings-Vorm in een Tydvak van 4500 Jaaren*.
Alkmaar, 1794. 156 p.

NN

421   Gesell, Silvio, 1862–1930.
      Freiland, die Eherne Forderung des Friedens. Erfurt, 1917.
      38 p.

      DLC NN   1921: MH

422   ————.
      The Truth, Revealing Economic Experiments of Barataria. San
      Antonio, Tex., 1938. 32 p.

      NcD NN

423   Gieske, Herman Everett.
      Utopia, Inc. New York, 1940. 223 p.

      CtY DLC MH NcD NN

424   [Gilbert, Claude], 1652–1720.
      Histoire de Calejava ou de l'Îsle des Hommes Raisonnables.
      Avec le Paralelle de Leur Morale et du Christianisme. Dijon,
      1700. 329 p.

      BN

425   [————].
      Extracts from *Histoire de Calejava* . . . in *Les Successeurs de*
      Cyrano de Bergerac, by Frédéric Lachèvre. Paris, 1922.

      BM CtY DLC ICN ICU NcD NN

426   Gilbert, John Wilmer, 1865–.
      The Marsian. New York, 1940. 156 p.

      DLC

427   Gilbert, Sir William Schwenck, 1836–1911, and Sir Arthur Seymour
      Sullivan, 1842–1900.
      Utopia, Limited; or, the Flowers of Progress. London, 1893.
      52 p.

      CSmH (with the score)   1893: BM CtY ICN NN
      Works: DLC ICU MH NcD

428   [Gildon, Charles] (*pseud.* Morris Williams), 1665–1724 (probable
      author).

"The Fortunate Shipwreck, or a Description of New Athens in Terra Australis Incognita . . . by Morris Williams." In *Miscellanea Aurea,* by Thomas Killigrew, chap. 2. London, 1720.

BM DLC ICN ICU MH

429   Giles, Fayette Stratton.
    Shadows Before, or, a Century Onward. New York, 1893. 286 p.

    ICU   1894: BM DLC

430   Gillette, King Camp, 1855–.
    World Corporation. Boston, 1910. 240 p.

    BM CSmH CtY DLC ICN ICU MH NcD NN

431   Gilman, Mrs. Charlotte (Perkins) Stetson, 1860–1935.
    Moving the Mountain. New York, 1911. 290 p.

    CSmH CtY DLC

432   Girardin, Georges.
    Vingt-Quatre Heures dans le Monde Nouveau. Comment on Vit dans la "Cité Intégration," Cité Sans Prolétariat. Rossigné, 1947. 155 p.

    BN NcD

433   ————.
    Vers un Monde Nouveau Immédiat; Comment Organiser une Vie Indépendante Sans Prolétariat. Paris, 1947. 32 p.

    BM BN MH

434   Gisander, Eberhard Julius (*pseud.*). *See* Schnabel, Johann Gottfried.

435   Gloag, John Edwards, 1896–.
    Tomorrow's Yesterday. London, 1932. 184 p.

    BM DLC NcD

436   Godfrey, Hollis, 1874–.
    The Man Who Ended War. Boston, 1908. 301 p.

    DLC MH NcD NN   1910: BM

437   [Godwin, Francis] (*pseud.* Domingo Gonsales), 1562–1633.
      The Man in the Moone: or a Discourse of a Voyage Thither.
      By Domingo Gonsales, the Speedy Messenger. London, 1638.
      126 p.

      BM BN CtY MH   1657: CSmH

438   [————].
      The Man in the Moone, and Nuncius Inanimatus. . . . Edited
      by Grant McColley. Northampton, Mass., 1937. 78 p.

      BM BN CtY DLC ICN ICU MH NcD NN

439   [————].
      The Man in the Moone. Edited by Ivan Volkoff. San Marino,
      Calif., 1961. 92 p.

      CSmH CtY DLC NcD

440   Goldsmith, John Francis.
      President Randolph as I Knew Him: an Account of the His-
      toric Events of the 1950's and 1960's Written from the Personal
      Experiences of the Secretary to the President. Philadelphia,
      1935. 448 p.

      DLC MH NcD NN

441   Goldsmith, Oliver, 1728–1774.
      "Asem, an Eastern Tale." In *Essays,* pp. 126–48. London, 1765.

      BM CtY DLC MH NcD   1766: NN   1792: ICN
      n.d.: BN   Works: CSmH ICU

442   Gómez de la Serna, Ramón, 1888–1963.
      La Utopia. Madrid, 1921. 36 p.

      NN   Works: ICU MH NcD

443   [Gompertz, Martin Louis Alan] (*pseud.* Ganpat), 1886–.
      Harilek, a Romance of Modern Central Asia. Edinburgh and
      London, 1923. 336 p.

      BM CtY DLC MH NcD NN

444   Gonsales, Domingo (*pseud.*). *See* Godwin, Francis.

445   González Casanova, Pablo, 1922–.
Una Utopia de America. Mexico City, 1953. 171 p.

BN CtY DLC MH NcD NN

446   Gonzalez Gallego, Serapio.
John Smith, Emperor. St. Paul, Minn., 1944. 160 p.

CtY DLC NcD NN

447   Gordon, Rex *(pseud.)*. *See* Hough, Stanley Bennett.

448   [Gott, Samuel], 1613–1671.
Novae Solymae libri sex. London, 1648. 391 p.

BM

449   [————].
Nova Solyma the Ideal City; or, Jerusalem Regained. Translated by Walter Begley. 2 vols. London, 1902. (Erroneously attributed by Begley to John Milton.)

BM BN CSmH CtY DLC ICN NcD NN

450   Gotthelf, Ezra Gerson, 1907–.
The Island of Not-Me. A True Chronicle of the Life of Geoghan Willbe on the Island of "Not-Me," Preceded by an Account of His Person Before his Arrival upon that Famous Isle. New York, 1935. 156 p.

DLC MH NcD NN

451   Graf, Oskar Maria, 1894–.
Die Eroberung der Welt. Roman einer Zukunft. Munich, 1948, 1949. 583 p.

CtY DLC ICU MH NcD NN

452   Graffigny, Henri de. *See* Le Faure, Georges.

453   Grave, Charles Joseph de, 1731–1805.
République des Champs Élysées, ou Monde, Ancien. 3 vols. Ghent, 1806.

BN   1957 (Dutch): DLC MH

454   Grave, Jean.
      La Société Future. Paris, 1895. 414 p.

      BM BN CtY ICU NcD

455   ————.
      Les Aventures de Nono. Paris, 1901. 372 p.

      BN ICU MH   1907 (Spanish): BM

456   ————.
      Terre Libre (les Pionniers). Paris, 1908. 324 p.

      BN CtY MH   1908 (Spanish): BM

457   Graves, Charles Larcom, 1856–1944, and Edward Verrall Lucas, 1868–1938.
      The War of the Wenuses. Translated from the Artesian of H. G. Pozzuoli. Bristol, 1898. 140 p.

      BM CtY ICN MH NcD

458   Graves, Robert von Ranke, 1895–.
      Seven Days in New Crete. London, 1949. 281 p. (Published in the U.S. as *Watch the North Wind Rise*. New York, 1949. 290 p.)

      BM CSmH CtY DLC ICN MH NcD NN

459   Green, Nunsowe (*pseud.*).
      A Thousand Years Hence. Being Personal Experiences as Narrated by Nunsowe Green, Esq. London, 1882. 397 p.

      BM

460   [Greener, William Oliver] (*pseud.* Wirt Gerrare), 1862–.
      The Warstock: a Tale of Tomorrow. London, 1898. 218 p.

      BM DLC

461   [Greenwood, Julia Eileen Courtney] (*pseud.* Francis Askham).
      The Heart Consumed. London, 1944. 234 p.

      BM DLC   1946 (French): BN

462   Greg, Percy, 1836–1889.
Across the Zodiac—the Story of a Wrecked Record, Deciphered,
Translated and Edited by Percy Greg. 2 vols. London, 1880.

BM DLC MH NcD

463   Gregorovius, Emil.
Der Himmel auf Erden in den Jahren 1901 bis 1912. Leipzig,
1892. 160 p.

BM ICN MH NN

464   Gregory, Owen.
Meccania, the Super-State. London, 1918. 298 p.

BM DLC ICN MH NcD

465   Grierson, Francis Durham, 1888–.
Heart of the Moon. London, 1928. 287 p.

BM DLC NcD

466   Griesser, Wilhelm.
The Welcome Island, Story and Laws. Chicago, 1923. 257 p.

DLC MH NcD NN

467   [Griffin, Anthony Jerome] (*pseud.* Altair), 1866–1935.
Chaos; a Vision of Eternity. New York, 1919. 55 p.

BM BN DLC ICU MH NcD NN

468   Griffith, George Chetwynd.
The Angel of the Revolution: a Tale of the Coming Terror.
London, 1893. 393 p.

BM NcD

469   Griffith, Mary, *d.* 1877.
Camperdown; or, News from Our Neighbourhood. Philadelphia, 1836. 300 p.

CSmH CtY ICN MH NcD

470 ——————.

Three Hundred Years Hence. Edited by Nelson F. Adkins. Philadelphia, 1950. 131 p.

CSmH CtY DLC NcD NN

471 Griffiths, Isabel.
Three Worlds. London, 1922. 198 p.

BM NcD

472 [Grigsby, Alcanoan O.] (pseud. Jack Adams).
Nequa; or, the Problem of the Ages. Topeka, Kan., 1900. 387 p.

BM DLC ICU NcD

473 Grisewood, Robert Norman, 1876–.
Zarlah, the Martian. New York, 1909. 194 p.

CtY DLC NcD NN

474 Grivel, Guillaume, 1735–1810.
L'Îsle Inconnue; ou Mémories du Chevalier des Gastines. 6 vols. Paris, 1783–87.

BM BN DLC ICU MH NcD   1787–93: CSmH ICN NN

475 Grogan, Gerald, 1884–1918.
A Drop in Infinity. London, 1915. 325 p.

BM CtY NcD NN

476 Gros de Besplas, l'abbe Joseph Marie, 1734–1783.
Le Rituel des Esprit-Forts, ou le Voyage d'Outre-Monde; en Forme de Dialogues. N.p., 1759. 168 p.

BN NcD

477 ——————.

Des Causes du Bonheur Public. Paris, 1768. 588 p.

BN Bod ICU MH NcD

478 Gubbins, Herbert.
The Elixir of Life; or, 2905 A.D. A Novel of the Far Future. London, 1914. 254 p.

BM NcD

479   Guest, Ernest.
        At the End of the World, a Vision. London, 1929. 112 p.
        BM

480   Guevara, Antonio de, 1474–1546.
        Libro Aureo de Marco Aurelio. Seville, 1527. 126 ff.
        1528: MH   1529: BM   1531: CSmH   1533: ICN ICU
        1539: BN   1540: CtY   1546: DLC   1647: NN

481   ————.
        The Golden Boke of Marcus Aurelius. Translated by John
        Bourchier, Lord Berners. London, 1534. 167 ff.
        1537: Bod CSmH   1539: BM   1542: ICN
        1553: ICU MH

482   ————.
        Libro di Marco Aurelio con l'Horologio de Principi. 4 vols. in 1.
        Venice, 1556.
        BM CtY   1568: ICN   1571: BN   1584: DLC NcD

483   ————.
        L'Orologe des Princes. Paris, 1540. 90–72–82 ff.
        BM BN MH   1576: NcD   1577: CtY   1608: ICU

484   ————.
        The Diall of Princes. Translated by Sir Thomas North. Lon-
        don, 1557. 268 ff.
        BM CSmH CtY ICN ICU MH   1582: DLC NN
        1619: NcD

485   ————.
        The Diall of Princes. Translated by Sir Thomas North. Edited
        by K. N. Colvile. London, 1919. 263 p.
        BM CSmH CtY DLC ICN MH NcD NN

486   ————.
        La Institutione del Princepi Christiano. Translated by Mam-
        brino Roseo de Fabriano. Venice, 1543. 178 ff.
        BM BN CtY ICN   1562: NcD

487   Gull, Cyril Arthur Edward Ranger, 1876–1923.
       The City in the Clouds. London, 1921. 288 p.

       BM DLC MH   1922: NcD

488   Gulliver, Captain (*pseud.*).
       Memoirs of the Court of Lilliput. Written by Captain Gulliver.
       Containing an Account of the Intrigues, and Some other Par-
       ticular Transactions of That Nation, Omitted in the Two Vol-
       umes of His Travels. London, 1727. 159 p.

       ICN MH

489   Gulliver, Dean (*pseud.*).
       The Land of Unreason. London, 1905. 148 p.

       BM

490   Gulliver, Jean. *See* Desfontaines, Pierre François Guyot.

491   Gulliver, Lemuel (*pseud.*). *See* Swift, Jonathan.

492   Gulliver, Lemuel (*pseud.*).
       Sequel to Gulliver's Travels. An Eulogy. London, 1830. 16 p.

       BM CSmH

493   Gulliver, Lemuel, jun. (*pseud.*). *See* Whitmore, H.

494   Gulliver Redivivus (*pseud.*).
       Laputa Revisited. London, 1905. 124 p.

       BM

495   Guthrie, Kenneth Sylvan, 1871–.
       A Romance of Two Centuries, a Tale of the Year 2025. Alpine,
       N.J., 1919. 365 p.

       BM CtY DLC MH NcD

496   Guttin, Jacques.
       Épigone, Histoire du Siècle Futur. Paris, 1659.

       BN

497   H., R.
       New Atlantis, Begun by the Lord Verulam, Viscount St. Albans' and Continued by R. H. Esquire, Wherein Is Set Forth a Platform of Monarchial Government, with a Pleasant Intermixture of Divers Rare Inventions, and Wholesom Customs, Fit to be Introduced into all Kingdoms, States, and Common-Wealths. London, 1660. 101 p.

       MH

498   Hake, William Augustus Gordon.
       Society Organized; an Allegory. London, 1840. 144 p.

       BM

499   Haldane, Charlotte (Franken), 1894–.
       Man's World. London, 1926. 299 p.

       BM DLC NcD   1927: MH NN

500   Hale, Edward Everett, 1822–1909.
       Col. Ingham's Visit to Sybaris. Boston, 1869. 206 p.

       MH NN

501   —————.
       Sybaris and Other Homes. Boston, 1869. 206 p.

       BM CSmH CtY DLC ICN ICU MH NcD

502   —————.
       Ten Times One is Ten: the Possible Reformation. By Col. Frederick Ingham. Boston, 1871. 148 p.

       CSmH CtY DLC ICU MH NcD NN   1899: ICN

503   —————.
       How They Lived in Hampton; a Study of Practical Christianity Applied in the Manufacture of Woolens. Boston, 1888. 281 p.

       CtY DLC ICN ICU MH NcD

504   Halévy, Daniel, 1872–.
       Histoire des Quatre Ans, 1997–2001. Paris, 1903. 143 p.

       BM BN CtY MH NcD

505 Hall, Harold Curtis (Hal Hall), 1911–.
The Great Conflict. Los Angeles, 1942. 151 p.
DLC ICU NN   1943: NcD

506 [Hall, Joseph], (*pseud.* Mercurio Britannico), 1574–1656.
Mundus Alter et Idem Sive Terra Australis Ante Hac Semper Incognita Longis Itineribus Peregrini Academici Nupperrime Lustrata, Authore Mercurio Britannico. Frankfurt (i.e., London), *ca.* 1605. 224 p.
BM CSmH CtY ICN MH NcD NN   1607: BN DLC
1643: ICU

507 [————].
The Discovery of a New World or a Description of the South Indies, Hetherto Unknowne. By an English Mercury. Translated by Joseph Healey. London, *ca.* 1609. 244 p.
BM CSmH ICN

508 [————].
The Discovery of a New World. Edited by Huntington Brown. Cambridge, 1937. 230 p.
BM CSmH CtY DLC ICN ICU MH NcD NN

509 Halle, Louis Joseph, 1910–.
Sedge. New York, 1963. 118 p.
CtY DLC ICU MH NcD

510 Halsbury, Hardinge Goulburn Giffard, earl of, 1880–.
1944. London, 1926. 302 p.
BM CtY DLC MH NcD NN

511 Hamada, Nobuya.
An Ideal World. Berlin, 1922. 144 p.
BM DLC NN

512 Hamilton, Cicely Mary, 1875–.
Theodore Savage: a Story of the Past or the Future. London, 1922. 320 p.
BM NcD

513 Hamilton, Patrick.
Impromptu in Moribundia. London, 1939. 288 p.
BM ICU NcD

514 Hamsun, Knut.
Markens Grøde. 2 vols. Copenhagen, 1917.
BM DLC MH NcD NN   1919: CtY ICU

515 ————.
The Growth of the Soil. Translated by W. Worster. London, 1920. 406 p.
BM CtY DLC MH NcD   1921: ICU NN

516 Harben, William Nathaniel, 1858–1919.
The Land of the Changing Sun. New York, 1894. 233 p.
CSmH CtY DLC NcD NN

517 Harding, Ellison.
The Demetrian. New York, 1907. 315 p.
BM DLC NcD NN

518 ————.
The Woman Who Vowed. London, 1908.
BM

519 [Harrington, James], 1611–1677.
The Common-Wealth of Oceana. London, 1656. 281 p.
BM BN CtY DLC ICN ICU MH   1700: CSmH
1737: NcD   1887: NN

520 [————].
Valerius and Publicola: or, the True Form of a Popular Commonwealth Extracted e puris naturalibus. London, 1659. 35 p.
(The preliminary draft of *The Rota*.)
BM Bod CSmH CtY MH   1700: ICN ICU   1737: NcD

521 [————].
The Rota; or, a Model of a Free-State, or Equall Commonwealth. London, 1660. 29 p.
BM CSmH CtY DLC ICN ICU MH NN   1737: NcD

522   [————].
     The Way and Means Whereby an Equal and Lasting Common-
     wealth May Be Suddenly Introduced and Perfectly Founded
     with the Free Consent and Actual Confirmation of the Whole
     People of England. London, 1660. 5 p.

     BM MH NN   1700: CtY ICN ICU
     1737: CSmH DLC NcD

523   [Harris, Edwin Ruthven], 1857–.
     The Universal Republic! 1992. A History of the Past, Present,
     and Future of the United States. St. Louis, 1891. 251 p.

     DLC

524   [Harris, John Beynon] (*pseud.* John Wyndham), 1903–.
     The Day of the Triffids. New York, 1951. 222 p.

     BM CtY DLC   1964: ICU NcD   1956 (French): BN

525   Harris-Burland, John Burland, 1870–.
     Dr. Silex. London, 1905. 158 p.

     BM NcD   1908: BN

526   Hart, Julius.
     Zukunftsland, im Kampf um eine Weltanschauung. 2 vols.
     Florence and Leipzig, 1899, 1902.

     BM

527   [Harting, Pieter] (*pseuds.* Dr. Dioscorides; Alexander V. W. Bik-
     kers), 1812–1885.
     Anno 2065: een Blik in de Toekomst, door Dr. D. Utrecht,
     1865.

     BM NN

528   [————].
     Anno Domini 2071. Translated from the Dutch . . . by Dr.
     A. V. W. Bikkers. London, 1871. 132 p.

     BM MH NcD

529   Hartley, Leslie Poles.
       Facial Justice. London, 1960. 256 p.
       BM CSmH DLC ICU MH NcD NN

530   [Hartlib, Samuel], *ca.* 1598–1662 or 1670.
       *A Description of the Famous Kingdom of Macaria; Showing
       Its Excellent Government . . . In a Dialogue Between a Scholar
       and a Traveller*. London, 1641. 15 p.
       BM CtY ICN ICU MH

531   [————].
       A Description of the Famous Kingdom. . . . Edited by Richard
       H. Dillon. Sausalito, Calif., 1961. 15 p.
       CSmH DLC ICN

532   Harton, Sir Robert (*pseud.*). *See* Walker, John Brisben.

533   Hartshorne, Henry, 1823–1897.
       1931: a Glance at the Twentieth Century. Philadelphia, 1881.
       64 p.
       BM NcD

534   Harvey, William Hope, 1851–1936.
       Paul's School of Statesmanship. Chicago, 1924. 184 p.
       DLC MH NcD NN

535   Hastings, George Gordon.
       The First American King. New York, 1904. 350 p.
       DLC NcD NN

536   Hatfield, Richard, 1853–.
       *Geyserland, Empiricisms in Social Reform; Being Data and
       Observations Recorded by the Late Mark Stubble, M.D., Ph.D.*
       Washington, 1908. 451 p.
       DLC ICN NcD NN

537   Hathaway, Hanson.
       *The Utopians Are Coming; a New Interpretation of Constitu-
       tional Americanism*. Hollywood, Calif., 1934. 64 p.
       DLC NcD NN

538   Hauptmann, Gerhart Johann Robert, 1862–1946.
Die Insel der Grossen Mutter; oder, das Wunden von Île des Dames; eine Geschichte aus dem Utopischen Archipelagus. Berlin, 1924. 373 p.

        BM BN CtY DLC ICN ICU NN   1925: MH NcD

539   ⸺.
The Island of the Great Mother, or, the Miracle of Île des Dames; a Story from the Utopian Archipelago. Translated by Willa and Edwin Muir. New York, 1925. 328 p.

        BM CSmH CtY DLC ICN MH NcD NN

540   Hay, William Delisle.
Three Hundred Years Hence; or, a Voice from Posterity. London, 1881. 356 p.

        BM CtY MH

541   Hayes, Frederick William.
The Great Revolution of 1905; or, the Story of the Phalanx. London, 1893. 316 p.

        BM ICN NcD

542   Hayes, Hiram Wallace, 1858–.
The Peacemakers. Boston, 1909. 420 p.

        BM DLC MH NcD NN

543   [Haywood, Mrs. Eliza (Fowler)], 1693(?)–1756.
Memoirs of a Certain Island Adjacent to Utopia. Written by a Celebrated Author of That Country. Now Translated into English. 2 vols. London, 1725.

        BM CSmH CtY ICN MH   1726: DLC NcD NN

544   Hazlitt, Henry, 1894–.
The Great Idea. New York, 1951. 374 p.

        BM CtY DLC ICN ICU MH NcD NN

545   Heard, Henry Fitzgerald (Gerald Heard), 1889–.
Doppelgangers; an Episode of the Fourth, the Psychological Revolution, 1997. New York, 1947. 281 p.

        CtY DLC MH NcD NN   1948: BM

546 [Hearn, Mary Ann] (*pseud.* Marianne Farningham).
Nineteen Hundred? A Forecast and a Story. London, 1892.
318 p.

BM NcD

547 [Hecht, Friedrich] (*pseud.* Manfred Langrenus), 1903–.
Reich im Mond; Utopisch-Wissenschaftlicher Roman aus Naher Zukunft und Jahrmillionenferner Vergangenheit. Leoben, 1951.
545 p.

DLC

548 Hellenbach, Lazar B., freiherr von, 1827–1887.
Die Insel Mellonta: ein Zukunftsbild. Vienna, 1883. 237 p.

BM   1896: DLC MH

549 [Helps, Sir Arthur], 1813–1875.
Realmah. 2 vols. London, 1868.

BM CSmH DLC ICN MH   1869: CtY ICU NcD NN

550 Hendow, Z. S.
The Future Power; or, the Great Revolution of 190–. Westminster, 1897. 79 p.

BM

551 [Henham, Ernest George] (*pseud.* John Trevena), 1870–.
The Reign of the Saints. London, 1911. 376 p.

BM DLC MH

552 [Henningsen, Charles Frederick], 1815–1877.
Sixty Years Hence. 3 vols. London, 1847.

Bod DLC   1848: MH

553 Henry, Walter O., 1858–.
Equitania; or the Land of Equity. Omaha, Nebr., 1914. 164 p.

CtY DLC ICN MH NcD NN

554 *Henry Russell; or, the Year of Our Lord Two Thousand.* New York, 1846. 115 p.

CtY NN

555   Herbert, Edward Geisler.
       Newaera: a Socialist Romance, with a Chapter on Vaccination.
       London, 1910. 212 p.

       BM ICN NcD NN

556   Herbert, William (*pseud.*). *See* Croly, Herbert David.

557   Hermes, Lumley B. (*pseud.*). *See* Lumley, Benjamin.

558   Herrick, Robert, 1868–1938.
       Sometime. New York, 1933. 338 p.

       DLC ICN ICU MH NcD

559   Hérrissant, Louis Théodore. *See* Palafox y Mendoza, Juan de.

560   Herrman, Louis.
       In the Sealed Cave: Being a Modern Commentary on a Strange
       Discovery Made by Captain Lemuel Gulliver in the Year 1721
       and Now Published from Manuscript Notes Recently Come to
       Light. London, 1935. 226 p.

       BM NcD NN

561   Hertzka, Theodor, 1845–1924.
       Freiland; ein Sociales Zukunftsbild. Dresden and Leipzig, 1890.
       330 p.

       BM BN CtY DLC ICN MH NcD NN

562   —————.
       Freeland; A Social Anticipation. Translated by Arthur Ran-
       som. London, 1891. 443 p.

       BM CtY DLC ICN ICU MH NcD NN

563   —————.
       "Freiland" und die Freilandbewegung. Dresden and Leipzig,
       1891. 64 p.

       BM NcD

564   —————.
       Eine Reise nach Freiland. Leipzig, 1893. 183 p.

       DLC ICN MH

565 ————.
A Visit to Freeland; or, the New Paradise Regained. London, 1894. 155 p.

BM NN   1905: CtY DLC

566 Hesse, Hermann, 1877–1962.
Das Glasperlenspiel. Versuch einer Lebensbeschreibung des Magister Ludi Josef Knecht Samt Knechts Hinterlassen Schriften. 2 vols. Zurich, 1943.

BM CtY DLC ICN ICU MH NcD NN   1952: CSmH
1961: BN

567 ————.
Magister Ludi. Translated by M. Savill. New York, 1949. 502 p.

CtY DLC ICU MH NcD NN   1950: BM

568 Heywood, D. Herbert.
Twentieth Century. A Prophecy of the Coming Age. Boston, 1890. 48 p.

DLC

569 Hicks, Granville, 1901–, and Richard M. Bennett.
The First to Awaken. New York, 1940. 346 p.

CtY DLC ICN ICU MH NcD NN

570 Hilton, James, 1900–1954.
Lost Horizon. New York, 1933. 277 p.

BM CtY DLC ICU   1934: ICN MH NcD NN
1939: BN

571 [Hird, James Dennis] (Dennis Hird), 1850–1920.
Toddle Island: Being the Diary of Lord Bottsford. London, 1894. 406 p.

BM MH

572 *Histoire de Camouflet, Souverain Potentat de L'Empire d'Équivopolis*. Équivopolis (i.e., Paris), 1751. 84 p.

BM ICN   1752: CtY

573   Hodgson, William, 1745–1851.
The Commonwealth of Reason. London, 1795. 104 p.

BM DLC ICN ICU NcD NN

574   Hodgson, William Hope, 1877–1918.
The Night Land. London, 1912. 583 p.

BM   1921: NcD   1946: ICN

575   [Holberg, baron Ludvig af] (*pseud.* Nicholas Klimius), 1684–1754.
Nicolai Klimii Iter Subterraneum Novam Telluris Theoriam ac Historiam Quintae Monarchiae Adhuc Nobis Incognitae Exhibens e Bibliotheca B. Abelini. Copenhagen and Leipzig, 1741. 380 p.

BM BN CSmH CtY DLC MH NcD

576   [————].
A Journey to the World Underground. London, 1742. 324 p.

BM CtY DLC ICN ICU MH NcD NN

577   [————].
A Journey to the World Underground. Edited by James I. McNelis, Jr. Lincoln, Neb., 1960. 236 p.

CtY DLC ICU MH NcD

578   Holford, Castello.
Aristopia; a Romance History of the New World. Boston, 1895. 234 p.

DLC

579   Holtby, Winifred, 1898–1935.
The Astonishing Island. Being a Veracious Record of the Experiences Undergone by Robinson Lippingtree Mackintosh from Tristan da Cunha During an Accidental Visit to Unknown Territory in the Year of Grace MCMXXX–? London, 1933. 184 p.

BM CSmH CtY DLC NcD NN

580   Homo, Dr. Ali (*pseud.*). *See* Hompf, Alois.

581   [Hompf, Alois] (*pseud.* Dr. Ali Homo).
       Neue Erde; den Völkern Gewidnet. Homoneion, Unitas Magna. Warmbrunn, 1938. 98 p.
       DLC

582   [Hone, William], 1780–1842 (attributed author).
       The Man in the Moon. (A Speech from the Throne to the Senate of Lunataria.) London, 1820. 24 p.
       BM CSmH CtY DLC ICN ICU MH   1827: NcD

583   [Hough, Stanley Bennett] (*pseud.* Rex Gordon).
       Utopia 239. London, 1955. 208 p.
       BM DLC NcD

584   [House, Edward Mandell], 1858–1938.
       Phillip Dru: Administrator; a Story of Tomorrow, 1920–1935. New York, 1912. 312 p.
       CtY DLC ICN MH NcD   1919: ICU   1920: NN

585   Hovorre, M. Auburre (*pseud.*). *See* Howard, Albert Waldo.

586   [Howard, Albert Waldo] (*pseud.* M. Auburre Hovorre).
       The Milltillionaire, or, the Age of Bardization. Boston, 1895. 30 p.
       DLC   19–: NN

587   Howard, Sir Ebenezer, 1850–1928.
       To-morrow—a Peaceful Path to Social Reform. London, 1898. 176 p.
       BM CtY DLC MH

588   ———.
       Garden Cities of Tomorrow. London, 1902. 167 p.
       BM CtY DLC ICU MH NcD NN   1917 (French): BN

589   [Howard, Edward], 1624–*ca.* 1700.
       The Six Days Adventure; or, the New Utopia, A Comedy. London, 1671. 84 p.
       BM Bod CSmH CtY DLC ICN ICU MH NN

590 Howell, James, 1594(?)–1666.
Δενδρολογία. *Dodona's Grove, or the Vocall Forrest.* London, 1640. 219 p.

BM BN CSmH CtY DLC ICN ICU MH NcD
1644: NN

591 ―――――.
Epistolae Ho-Elianae . . . Familiar Letters Domestic and Forren . . . Partly Historicall, Politicall, Philosophicall. London, 1645. 510 p.

BM CSmH CtY ICN MH   1650: BN ICU NcD NN
1688: DLC

592 ―――――.
Θηρολογία. *The Parly of Beasts; or, Morphandra Queen of the Inchanted Island.* London, 1660. 152 p.

BM CSmH CtY DLC ICN ICU MH NN

593 Howells, William Dean, 1837–1920.
A Traveler from Altruria. New York, 1894. 318 p.

BM CSmH CtY DLC ICN ICU MH NcD NN

594 ―――――.
Through the Eye of the Needle. New York and London, 1907. 232 p.

BM CSmH CtY DLC ICN ICU MH NcD NN

595 Howland, Marie.
Papa's Own Girl; a Novel. New York and Boston, 1874. 547 p.
[Third edition published as *The Familistere; a Novel.* Boston, 1918.]

CtY DLC MH NN

596 Hudson, William Henry, 1841–1922.
A Crystal Age. London, 1887. 316 p.

BM CSmH CtY DLC MH   1906: NN   1916: ICN
1917: ICU NcD   1919: BN

597   *Human Vicissitudes; or, Travels into Unexplored Regions.* 2 vols.
        London, 1798.

        MH

598   [Hume, Ferguson Wright] (Fergus Hume), 1859–1932.
        *The Year of Miracle: a Tale of the Year One Thousand Nine
        Hundred.* London, 1891. 148 p.

        BM DLC

599   [————].
        The Island of Fantasy; a Romance. London, 1892. 453 p.

        BM DLC   1905: NcD

600   Hunt, Haroldson Lafayette.
        Alpaca. Dallas, Tex., 1960. 183 p.

        CtY DLC NcD NN

601   ————.
        Gobiernate a Ti Mismo. Dallas, Tex., 1961. 28 p.

        NcD

602   Huxley, Aldous Leonard, 1894–1963.
        Brave New World. London, 1932. 306 p.

        BM BN CSmH CtY DLC ICN ICU MH NcD NN

603   ————.
        Ape and Essence. New York, 1948. 205 p.

        BN CSmH CtY DLC ICN ICU MH NcD NN
        1949: BM

604   ————.
        Brave New World Revisited. New York, 1958. 147 p.

        CSmH CtY DLC ICN ICU MH NcD
        1959: BM BN NN

605   ————.
        Island. London, 1962. 286 p.

        BM BN CSmH CtY DLC ICU MH NcD NN

606   Inca, El. *See* Garcilaso de la Vega.

607   Inciarte La-Barca, Israel.
        De Regreso de Marte. Valencia, Venezuela, 1957. 142 p.
        Bod DLC MH

608   *In the Future, A Sketch in Ten Chapters.* Hampstead, Eng., 1875.
        104 p.
        CtY NN

609   Inveni, Felix.
        Erwachsene Menschheit; ein Lebensbild des 26 Jahrhunderts.
        Bern, 1956. 293 p.
        CtY DLC NcD

610   Invisible Sam (*pseud.*). *See* Vose, Reuben.

611   *The Island of Atlantis. A Personal Narrative of the Travels and
        Wonderful Adventures of Lord Arthur A——Y, of Phantom
        Castle Ben Nevis.* London, 1871. 59 p.
        DLC NcD

612   Islet, Theodore Oceanic (*pseud.*). *See* Crocker, Samuel.

613   Izquierdo Croselles, Joaquin, 1878–.
        Lo Noche Encantada. Madrid, 1931. 188 p.
        DLC Biblioteca Nacional, Madrid

614   Jacomb, Charles Ernest, 1888–.
        And a New Earth. London, 1926. 239 p.
        BM NcD

615   Jaeger, Muriel.
        The Question Mark. New York, 1926. 249 p.
        BM DLC ICN NcD NN

616   [Jaffe, Hyman] (*pseud.* Alterego), 1882–.
Abdera, and the Revolt of the Asses. New York, 1937. 199 p.

DLC ICN NcD NN

617   Jefferies, (John) Richard, 1848–1887.
After London, or, Wild England. London, Paris, New York and Melbourne, 1885. 442 p.

BM BN CtY DLC ICN MH NcD NN   1906: ICU

618   [Jenkins, John Edward], 1838–1910.
Little Hodge. London, 1872. 108 p.

BM MH   1873: CtY NN

Nein, die Welt der Angeklagten. Hamburg, 1950. 277 p.
619   Jens, Walter, 1923–.

BM ICU MH NN

620   Johns, Willy.
The Fabulous Journey of Hieronymus Meeker. Boston, 1954. 370 p.

DLC MH NcD

621   Johnson, F. Hernaman.
The Polyphemes. A Story of Strange Adventures Among Strange Beings. London, 1906. 318 p.

BM

622   Johnson, Owen McMahon, 1878–.
The Coming of the Amazons; a Satiristic Speculation on the Scientific Future of Civilization. New York, 1931. 251 p.

BM CtY DLC MH NcD NN

623   Johnson, Samuel, 1709–1784.
[Rasselas.] The Prince of Abissinia. A Tale. 2 vols. London, 1759.

BM BN CSmH CtY DLC ICN MH NcD   1787: NN
1816: ICU

624   [Johnstone, Charles] (Johnson), 1719(?)–1800(?).
The Reverie: or, a Flight to the Paradise of Fools . . . By the Editor of The Adventures of a Guinea. 2 vols. Dublin, 1762.

BM CSmH CtY DLC MH   1763: ICN ICU NcD
1767: NN

625   [Jones, Alice Ilgenfritz, *d.* 1906, and Ella Merchant] (supposed authors).
Unveiling a Parallel. A Romance. By Two Women of the West. Boston, 1893. 269 p.

CSmH CtY NcD

626   Jouglet, René, 1884–.
Voyage à la République des Piles. Paris, 1928. 240 p.

BM BN DLC NN

627   Junius Secundus (*pseud.*). *See* Kelsall, Charles.

628   Justi, Johann Heinrich Gottlob von, 1720–1771.
Die Dichterinsul nach Ihren Verschiedenen Landschaften und dienen Darinnen Befindlichen Städten und Einwornern Sowohl als nach Dererselben Gottesdienst, Staats- und Kriegsverfassung Unpartheyisch Beschrieben Benebst einem Lobund Heldengedichte. Leipzig, 1745.

CtY ICU

629   Justinus, Oscar.
In der Zehn Millionen-Stadt. Dresden and Leipzig, 1890.

MH

630   *Justus en de Eilanders. Ein Fragment.* N.p., 1794. 128 p.

NN

631   Kayser, Mrs. Martha (Cabanné).
The Aerial Flight to the Realm of Peace. St. Louis, 1922. 54 p.

DLC NN

632   Kearney, Chalmers, 1881–.
      Erōne. Guildford, Eng., 1943. 253 p.
      BM CtY DLC NcD NN

633   [Kelsall, Charles] (*pseud.* Junius Secundus).
      Constantine and Eugene, or, an Evening at Mt. Vernon. Brussels, 1818. 252 p.
      BM CSmH DLC NN

634   Kendall, John (*pseud.*). *See* Brash, Margaret Maud.

635   Kernahan, John Coulson (Coulson Kernahan), 1858–1943.
      A World Without a Child: a Story for Women and for Men.
      London, New York, and Chicago, 1905. 64 p.
      BM DLC

636   Kerr, Frank Robinson, 1889–.
      Days After Tomorrow, a Voice from 2000 A.D. Melbourne,
      1944. 85 p.
      NN

637   [Killigrew, Thomas] (*pseud.* Morris Williams), 1612–1683 (probable author).
      "A Voyage to the Mountains of the Moon." In *Miscellanea Aurea,* pp. 1–34. London, 1720.
      BM CtY DLC ICN ICU

638   [King, William], 1663–1712.
      "A Voyage to the Island of Cajamai in America. Giving a Brief Account of the Natural Rarities, Inhabitants and Diseases of the Country . . . Translated into English from the Dutch." In *Useful Transactions in Philosophy, and Other Sorts of Learning.* London, 1709. 58 p.
      BM CtY DLC MH NN

639   [————].
      "A Voyage. . . ." In *The Original Works of William King,*
      2:132–78. London, 1776.
      BM CtY DLC ICN ICU MH NcD NN

640   Kipling, Rudyard, 1865–1936.
"With the Night Mail." In *Actions and Reactions,* pp. 109–69. London, 1909.

BM BN CSmH CtY DLC ICN ICU MH NcD NN

641   ————.
"As Easy as A B C." In *A Diversity of Creatures,* pp. 1–44. London, 1917.

BM BN CSmH CtY DLC ICN ICU MH NcD NN

642   [Kirwan, Thomas] (*pseud.* William Wonder), 1829–1911.
Reciprocity . . . in the Thirtieth Century. New York, 1908. 217 p.

DLC MH NN   1909: NcD

643   Klimius, Nicholas (*pseud.*). *See* Holberg, baron Ludvig af.

644   [Knight, Cornelia], 1757–1837.
Dinarbas; a Tale: Being a Continuation of Rasselas, Prince of Abyssinia. London, 1790. 336 p.

BM CSmH CtY DLC ICN MH NcD   1792: ICU
1795: NN

645   Knox, Ronald Arbuthnott, 1888–1957.
Memories of the Future: Being Memoirs of the Years 1915–1972, Written in the Year of Grace 1988 by Opal, Lady Porstock. London, 1923. 244 p.

BM BN CtY DLC ICN MH NcD NN

646   Koebel, William Henry, 1872–1923.
The Singular Republic. London, 1908. 335 p.

BM

647   [Korn, Friedrich] (*pseud.* F. Nork), 1803–1850.
Die Seleniten, oder die Mondbewohner wie Sie Sind. Aus den Papieren eines Luftseglers. Herausgegeben von F. Nork. Leipzig, 1835. 238 p.

BM

648   Kuppord, Skelton (*pseud.*). *See* Adams, J.

649   Laicus, Philipp (*pseud.*). *See* Wasserburg, Philipp.

650   *Das Lalebuch. Wunderseltsame, Abenteurerliche, Unerhörte und Bisher Unbeschriebene Geschicten und Thaten der Lalen zu Lalenburg in Misnopotamia Hinter Utopia Gelegen. Gedruckt zu Laleburg, 1597.* Stuttgart, 1839. 149 p.

    BM CtY MH

651   ————.

    Das Lalebuch. . . . Edited by Karl von Bahder. Halle, 1914. 198 p.

    BM CtY DLC ICN ICU MH NcD NN

652   La Liborlière. *See* Béllin de la Liborlière.

653   [Lambert, Claude François, abbé], 1705–1765.
    Le Nouveau Télémaque; ou Voyages et Aventures. 3 vols. The Hague, 1741.

    MH   1744: BN

654   [Lancetti, Vincenzo], 1767(?)–1851.
    Areostiade, Ossia il Mongolfiero. 2 vols. Milan, 1803.

    BM CSmH DLC NcD

655   Landis, Simon Mohler.
    An Entirely New Feature of a Thrilling New Novel! Entitled, the Social War of the Year 1900; or, the Conspirators and Lovers! Philadelphia, 1872. 416 p.

    CSmH CtY ICN NcD NN   1873: MH

656   [Lane, Mrs. Mary E. (Bradley).]
    Mizora: a Prophecy. A Mss. [*sic*] *Found Among the Private Papers of the Princess Vera Zarovitch. Being a True and Faithful Account of Her Journey to the Interior of the Earth, with a Careful Description of the Country and its Inhabitants, Their*

Customs, Manners and Government. Written by Herself. New York, 1890. 312 p.

1975: DLC NcD NN

657   Langrenus, Manfred *(pseud.)*. *See* Hecht, Friedrich.

658   LaPierre, Jean de.
Le Grand Empire de l'Un et l'Autre Mond Divisé en Trois Royaumes: le Royaume des Aveugles, des Borgnes, & des Clair-Voyants. Paris, 1625. 565 p.

BM BN ICN

659   [La Porte, Joseph de, abbé], 1713–1779.
Voyage au Séjour des Ombres. The Hague, 1749. 206 p.

BN ICN   1751: BM

660   [————].
Voyage en l'Autre Monde, ou Nouvelle Litteraires de Celui-cy. 2 vols. London, 1751.

BN   1752: ICN NN

661   Lasswitz, Kurd, 1848–1910.
Bilder aus der Zukunft . . . Zwei Erzählungen aus dem Vierundzwanzigsten und Neununddreissigsten Jahrhundert. 2 vols. Breslau, 1878.

DLC MH

662   *The Last Man; or, Omegarus and Syderia; a Romance in Futurity.* 2 vols. London, 1806.

BM CtY

663   Lawrence, James Cooper.
The Year of Regeneration; an Improbable Fiction. New York and London, 1932. 220 p.

BM DLC ICU MH NcD NN

664   Lawrence, Sir James Henry, 1773–1840.
The Empire of the Nairs; or, the Rights of Women. An Utopian Romance. 4 vols. London, 1811.

BM CtY DLC MH   1923 (German): ICN

665   Lawson, George, *d.* 1678.
Politica Sacra & Civilis, or a Modell of Civil and Ecclesiasticall Government. London, 1660. 264 p. London, 1689. 455 p.

1660: BM BN   1689: CtY ICN NcD NN

666   Lazarus, Henry.
The English Revolution of the 20th Century: a Prospective History. London, 1894. 463 p.

BM BN DLC ICN ICU MH NcD NN

667   Leacock, Stephen Butler, 1869–1944.
Afternoons in Utopia. New York, 1932. 221 p.

BM DLC ICN NcD NN

668   Leante, Eugenio.
Naaranuk; la Ciudad Encantada, la Ciudad Sagrada, la Ciudad Campestre, la Ciudad Feliz, en las Montañas Himalayas. Havana (?), 1944. 30 p.

DLC

669   Lee, Maj. Gen. Charles, 1731–1782.
"Sketch of a Plan for the Formation of a Military Colony." (Probably written 1779.) In *Memoirs of the Life of the Late Charles Lee, Esq. . . . To Which Are Added, His Political and Military Essays . . .* , edited by Edward Langworthy, pp. 48–55. Dublin, London, and New York, 1792.

BM BN CSmH CtY DLC ICN ICU MH NN
1793: NcD

670   Lee, Day Kellogg, 1876–.
The Master Builder; or, Life at a Trade. New York, 1852. 322 p.

BM CSmH CtY ICN MH NcD NN

671   Lee, Gerald Stanley, 1862–.
Inspired Millionaires; a Forecast. Northampton, Mass., 1908. 308 p.

BM CSmH CtY DLC ICU MH NcD NN

672   [Lee, Henry Boyle] (*pseud*. Theophilus McCrib).
        Kennaquhair. A Narrative of Utopian Travel. London, 1872.
        335 p.
        BM ICN NN

673   Le Faure, Georges and Henri de Graffigny.
        Aventures Extraordinaires d'un Savant Russe. Paris, 1889. 490 p.
        BM BN NN

674   Legge, James Granville, 1861–.
        The Millenium. Oxford, 1927. 163 p.
        BM

675   Leggett, Mortimer Dormer, 1821–1896.
        A Dream of a Modest Prophet. Philadelphia, 1890. 207 p.
        BM CSmH NcD

676   Le Grand, Antoine (Antonius Le Grand) *d*. 1699.
        Scydromedia, Seu Sermo, Quem Alphonsus de la Vida Habuit
        Coram Comite de Falmouth, de Monarchia. London, 1669.
        116 p.
        BM Bod   1680: BN MH

677   Leguat, François. *See* Misson, François Maximilien.

678   Le Mercier. *See* Mercier de la Rivière.

679   Leonhart, Raphael W. (*pseud*.). *See* Wybraniec, Peter Frank.

680   L'Épy, Héliogène de.
        A Voyage into Tartary, Containing a Curious Description of
        That Country, With Parts of Greece and Turkey, the Manners,
        Opinions, and Religion of the Inhabitants Therein. London,
        1689. 192 p.
        BM BN

681   Lerche, Julius, 1867–.
        Der Güterberg: Briefe aus dem Lande der Arbeit und der
        Arbeitsfreude. Stuttgart, 1922. 149 p.
        DLC

682   [Lesconvel, Pierre de], 1650–1722.

Idée d'un Regne Doux et Heureux, ou Relation du Voyage du Prince de Montberaud dans l'Île de Naudely. Caseres (i.e., Paris), 1703. 164 p.

BM DLC

[Other editions have varying titles: *Voyage l'Îsle de Naudely,* etc.]

683   [————].

Nouvelle Relation du Voyage du Prince de Montberaud, dans l'Îsle de Naudely. Ou Sont Rapportées Toutes les Maximes Qui Forment l'Harmonie d'un Parfait Gouvernement. Merinde, 1706. 388 p.

BM BN CtY ICN ICU MH NcD

684   Le Sueur, Théodore, *fl.* 1792.

Idées sur l'Espèce de Gouvernement Populaire . . . Essai Présenté à la Convention Nationale, par un Citoyen. Paris, 1792. 62 p.

BM BN

685   ————.

A French Draft Constitution of 1792 Modelled on James Harrington's Oceana. Edited by S. B. Liljegren. Lund, 1932. 180 p.

BM BN CSmH CtY DLC ICN ICU MH NcD NN

686   *Lettres d'Isaac à Mathieu. Dans Toutes les Capitales. En Tous les Siècles.* N.p., *ca.* 1760.

ICN

687   [Lewandowski, Herbert] (*pseud.* Lee van Dovski), 1896–.

Eine Reise ins Jahr 3000, Bericht eines Phantastischen Abenteuers. Zurich, 1951. 300 p.

CtY DLC MH   1952: NN   n.d.: BN

688   Lewis, Dewitt F.

A Trip to the North Pole and Beyond to Civilization. Linwood, Kan., 1912. 96 p.

NN

689   Lewis, Henry.
       The Way Out. The Social Revolution in Retrospect, Viewed from A.D. 2050. London, 1933. 60 p.

       BM NN

690   Liborlière, Béllin de la. *See* Béllin de la Liborlière.

691   Ligne, Charles Joseph, prince de, 1735–1814.
       "Utopie, ou Règne du Grand Selrahcengil." In *Oeuvres Choisies, Littéraires, Historiques et Militaires du Marechal Prince de Ligne,* vol. 1. Geneva, 1809.

       BM BN NcD

692   Lin, Yu-t'ang, 1895–.
       Looking Beyond. New York, 1955. 387 p.

       DLC ICU MH NcD NN

693   Lindsay, David, 1876–1945.
       Voyage to Arcturus. London, 1920. 303 p.

       BM DLC MH

694   —————.
       Voyage to Arcturus. London and New York, 1963. 244 p.

       BM BN NcD NN

695   Lister, Stephen (*pseud.*).
       Hail Bolonia! London, 1948. 170 p.

       BM

696   Listonai (*pseud.*). *See* Villeneuve, de.

697   Llewellyn, David William Alun.
       The Strange Invaders. London, 1934. 309 p.

       BM NcD

698   Lloyd, John Uri, 1849–1936.
       Etidorpha; or, the End of the Earth. The Strange History of a Mysterious Being and the Account of a Remarkable Journey,

as Communicated in Manuscript to Llewelyn Drury Who Promised to Print the Same, but Finally Evaded the Responsibility, Which Was Assumed by John Uri Lloyd. Cincinnati, 1895. 376 p. (Some editions are entitled *Etidorhpa.*)

BM CtY DLC ICN ICU NcD   1896: CSmH
1901: MH

699   Lloyd, John William, 1857–.
The Natural Man; a Romance of the Golden Age. Newark, N.J., 1902. 140 p.

DLC MH NcD

700   ————.
The Dwellers in Vale Sunrise; How They Got Together and Lived Happy Ever After. A Sequel to "The Natural Man." Westwood, Mass., 1904. 195 p.

DLC MH NcD NN

701   Lockhart-Mummery, John Percy, 1875–.
After Us, or the World As It Might Be. London, 1936. 287 p.

BM DLC NcD NN

702   Löwenthal, Josef, freiherr von, 1873–.
Die Unsterbliche Stadt; eine Utopische Erzählung aus dem Jahre 2000. Berlin, 1936. 266 p.

DLC

703   London, Jack, 1876–1916.
The Iron Heel. New York and London, 1908 [c. 1907]. 354 p.

BM CSmH CtY DLC ICN MH NcD   1913: BN
1917: ICU NN

704   Long, George.
Valhalla. London, 1906. 280 p.

BM   19–: NcD

705   Lookup, Alexander (*pseud.?*).
       Excelsior: or the Heir Apparent. New York and London, 1860.
       108 p.

       CSmH DLC ICU MH NN

706   ————.
       *The Soldier of the People; or the World's Deliverer. A Ro-
       mance.* New York, 1860. 108 p.

       DLC ICU MH NN

707   Lord Commissioner (*pseud.*). *See* McCoy, John.

708   [Loudon, Mrs. Jane (Webb)], 1807–1858.
       The Mummy! A Tale of the Twenty-Second Century. 3 vols.
       London, 1827.

       BM ICU   1828: CtY DLC MH

709   Lucas, Edward Verrall. *See* Graves, Charles Larcom.

710   [Lumley, Benjamin] (*pseud.* Lumley B. Hermes), 1812–1875.
       Sirenia; or, Recollections of a Past Existence. London, 1862.
       388 p.

       BM CtY NN

711   [————].
       *Another World; or, Fragments from the Star City of Montal-
       luyah.* London, 1873. 306 p.

       BM DLC NcD

712   Lunatic, Sir Humphrey, Bart. (*pseud.*). *See* Gentleman, Francis.

713   [Lupton, Thomas], *fl.* 1583.
       *Siuqila. Too Good to Be True . . . Herein Is Shewed by Waye
       of Dialoge, the Wonderfull Manners of the People of Mauqsun,
       with Other Talke not Frivolous.* London, 1580. 178 p.

       BM CSmH CtY ICN MH

714   [————].
      The Second Part . . . Wherein Is Continued the Discourse of the Wonderfull Lawes, of the People of Mauqsun. London, 1581. 207 p.

      BM CSmH CtY

715   Lynch, Arthur Alfred, 1861–.
      Seraph Wings. London, 1923. 318 p.

      BM DLC NcD

716   Lytton, Edward George Earle Bulwer, 1st baron, 1803–1873.
      The Coming Race: or the New Utopia. London, 1871. 292 p.

      BM CtY DLC ICN MH NcD   1873: BN NN
      1875: CSmH   Works: ICU

717   M******. *See* Morelly, abbé.

718   M. (I. D., G[entilhomme] T[ourangeau]).
      Histoire du Grand et Admirable Royaume d'Antangil . . . Avec la Description d'Icelui, & de Sa Police Nom-Pareille, Tant Civile Que Militaire. Saumur, 1616. 203 p.

      BM BN ICN

719   ————.
      Le Royaume d'Antangil. Edited by Frédéric Lachèvre. Paris, 1933. 162 p.

      BM ICN NcD NN

720   M., W.
      The Man in the Moone . . . or, the English Fortune-Teller. London, 1609.

      BM

721   ————.
      The Man in the Moone. . . . Edited by J. O. Halliwell. London, 1849. 56 p.

      BM CSmH CtY DLC ICN ICU MH NcD

722   Macaulay, Dame Rose.
        What Not; a Prophetic Comedy. London, 1918. 236 p.

        BM CSmH   1919: CtY DLC NN

723   ————.
        Orphan Island. London, 1924. 322 p.

        BM CSmH DLC NcD   1925: CtY ICU MH NN
        1945 (French): BN

724   [McCoy, John] (*pseud.* Lord Commissioner).
        A Prophetic Romance, Mars to Earth. Boston, 1896. 283 p.

        DLC

725   McCrib, Theophilus (*pseud.*). *See* Lee, Henry Boyle.

726   McDermot, Murtagh (*pseud.*).
        A Trip to the Moon. Dublin and London, 1728. 90 p.

        BM ICN NcD

727   Macdonald, William Allan.
        The World to Go and the World to Come; an Interview. London, 1907. 32 p.

        BM

728   McGrady, Thomas, Father, 1863–.
        Beyond the Black Ocean. Chicago, 1901. 304 p.

        DLC ICN ICU NN

729   [MacKay, Charles], 1814–1889.
        Baron Grimbosh, Doctor of Philosophy, and Sometime Governor of Barataria. A Record of His Experience. London, 1872. 293 p.

        BM MH NcD

730   Macleod, Hamish (*pseud.*).
        Across the Moon. London, 1924. 286 p.

        BM   1925: DLC NN

731   Macleod, Joseph Todd Gordon, 1903–.
        Overture to Cambridge. London, 1936. 264 p.
        BM NcD

732   [Macnie, John] (*pseud.* Ismar Thiusen), 1836–1909.
        The Diothas, or a Far Look Ahead. New York, 1883, 1890.
        Looking Forward; or, the Diothas. London, 1890. 358 p.
        BM CtY DLC ICN ICU NcD NN

733   Madariaga, Salvador de, 1886–.
        La Jirafa Sagrada, o el Buho de Plata. Madrid, 1925. 320 p.
        BM DLC NcD   1931: ICU   1941: CtY MH
        1953: BN

734   ————.
        The Sacred Giraffe. London, 1925. 269 p.
        BM BN CtY DLC ICN ICU MH NcD NN

735   [Madden, Samuel], 1686–1765.
        *Memoirs of the Twentieth Century. Being Original Letters of
        State under George the Sixth . . . Revealed in the Year 1728. In
        Six Volumes,* vol. 1. London, 1733. 31 + 527 p. (No other
        volumes were published.)
        BM CSmH CtY DLC ICN MH NN

736   ————.
        *The Reign of George VI, 1900–1925; a Forecast Written in the
        Year 1763.* London, 1763. 11 + 192 p.
        BM DLC

737   ————.
        The Reign of George VI. . . . Edited by C. Oman. London,
        1899. 110 p.
        BM DLC

738   [Madrazo, Federico de], 1815–1894 (probable author).
        *Astolfo, viages a un mondo desconocido, su historia, leyes y
        costumbres. Obra original. Por D. F. de M.* 2 vols. Madrid,
        1838.
        BM NcD

739 Magnus, Leonard Arthur.
    A Japanese Utopia. London, 1905. 131 p.
    BM ICN MH NN

740 Maguire, John Francis, 1815–1872.
    The Next Generation. 3 vols. London, 1871.
    BM ICU

741 Maitland, Edward, 1824–1897.
    By and By. An Historical Romance of the Future. New York and London, 1873. 460 p.
    Bod CtY DLC MH NcD   1876: ICN

742 [Mallock, William Hurrell], 1849–1923.
    The New Republic: or, Culture, Faith, and Philosophy in an English Country House. 2 vols. London, 1877.
    BM CtY DLC MH NN   1878: ICN   1880: NcD   1908: ICU

743 —————.
    The New Republic. . . . Edited with notes and an introduction by J. Max Patrick. Gainesville, Fla., 1950. 237 p.
    Bod CtY DLC ICU MH NcD NN

744 [Manley, Mary de la Riviere], 1663–1724.
    Secret Memoirs and Manners of Several Persons of Quality . . . From the New Atalantis. 2 vols. London, 1709.
    BM CtY ICU MH NcD   1717: DLC

745 Mann, Klaus Heinrich Thomas, 1906–1949.
    Alexander. Roman der Utopie. Berlin, 1930. 250 p.
    CtY DLC MH NcD NN   1931 (French): BN   1963: ICU

746 —————.
    Alexander. A Novel of Utopia. Translated by Marion Saunders. New York, 1930. 322 p.
    CtY DLC MH NcD NN

747   Mannin, Ethel Edith, 1900–.
Bread and Roses, An Utopian Survey and Blue-Print. London, 1944. 192 p.

BM CtY NcD   1945: DLC MH NN

748   Mantegazza, Paolo, 1831–1910.
L'Anno 3000. Milan, 1897. 328 p.
BM BN MH NcD NN

749   [Marquez y Espejo, D. Antonio, *b.* 1762] (probable author).
Viage de un Filósofo á Selenópolis, corte Desconocida de los Habitantes de la Tierra, Escrito por él Mismo, y Publicado por D. A. M. y E. Madrid, 1804. 182 p.

NcD

750   Marquis, Don (Donald Robert Perry), 1878–1937.
The Almost Perfect State. New York and London, 1927. 223 p.

BM CSmH CtY DLC ICN ICU MH NcD NN

751   Marshall, Archibald (Arthur Hammond), 1866–1934.
Upsidonia. London and New York, 1915. 286 p.

Bod CSmH NcD   1917: CtY DLC ICN ICU MH NN

752   Martin, Victoria (Claflin) Woodhull, 1838–1927.
A Page of American History. Constitution of the United States of the World. Cheltenham, Eng., 1870. 23 p.

NN

753   Massé, Jaques (*pseud.*). *See* Tyssot de Patot, Simon.

754   Masson, Émile, 1869–.
Utopia des Îles Bienheureuses dans le Pacifique en l'An 1980. Paris, 1921. 221 p.

BM BN CtY DLC ICN MH NcD NN

755   Mastin, John.
The Immortal Light. London, 1907. 307 p.

BM NcD

756   Matthews, Carleton.
        Flight to Utopia. Trenton, N.J., 1947. 209 p.

        CtY DLC MH NcD NN

757   Mauclair, Camille, 1872–.
        L'Orient Vierge. Roman Épique de l'An 2000. Paris, 1897. 317 p.

        BN CtY NcD   190–: MH   1920: BM

758   Maurois, André, 1885–.
        Voyage au Pays des Articoles. Paris, 1927. 134 p.

        MH   1928: BM BN CtY DLC NN

759   ————.
        A Voyage to the Island of the Articoles. Translated by David Garnett. New York, 1929. 75 p.

        BM CSmH CtY DLC ICN ICU MH NcD NN

760   Mawson, L. A.
        Methods from Mars. London, 1913. 208 p.

        BM

761   Maxton, James, 1885–1946.
        If I Were Dictator. London, 1935. 109 p.

        BM DLC ICU MH NcD NN

762   Mayo, William Starbuck, 1812–1895.
        Kaloolah, or Journeyings to the Djébel Kumri: an Autobiography of Jonathan Romer. Edited by W. S. Mayo, M.D. New York and London, 1849. 514 p.

        CtY DLC ICN MH NcD NN   1851: BM   1867: ICU

763   Mazade, André.
        "Au Pays de Liberté: une République Ideale." In *Nouvelle Revue* (Paris) 4 (1900):411–37 (new series).

        BM BN CtY DLC ICN ICU MH NcD NN

764   Mazeline, Guy.
        Les Îles du Matin. Paris, 1936. 343 p.

        BM CtY DLC MH NcD NN

765   Mears, Amelia Garland.
        Mercia, the Astronomer Royal. London, 1895. 349 p.

        BM NcD

766   [Meeker, Nathan Cook] (*pseud.* Capt. Jacob D. Armstrong), 1817–
        1879.
        Life and Adventures of Capt. Jacob D. Armstrong. New York,
        1852. 77 p.

        ICU NN

767   [Mehring, Daniel Gottlieb Gebhard.]
        *Das Jahr 2500 oder der Traum Alradi's. Aus einer Arabischen
        Handschrift des Sechszehnten Jahrhunderts.* 2 vols. Berlin,
        1794–95.

        BM

768   Melling, Leonard.
        The Great Beyond, A.D. 2500 . . . A Trilogy on Progress. Man-
        chester, Eng., 1955. 100 p.

        BM

769   Mendes, H[enry] Pereira.
        Looking Ahead. Twentieth Century Happenings. New York
        and London, 1899. 381 p.

        BM CtY DLC NcD NN

770   Menotti del Picchia, Paulo, 1892–.
        A Republica 3000. Romance. São Paulo, 1930. 253 p.

        DLC NcD NN   1950 (French): BN

771   Merchant, Ella. *See* Jones, Alice Ilgenfritz.

772   [Mercier, Louis Sébastien], 1740–1814.
        L'An Deux Mille Quatre Cent Quarante. Réve s'il Fût Jamais.
        Amsterdam, 1771. 416 p.

        BN Bod MH   1772: BM CtY ICN ICU NcD NN
        1775: DLC   1786: CSmH

773   [————].
        Memoirs of the Year Two Thousand Five Hundred. Translated
        by W. Hooper. 2 vols. London, 1772; Philadelphia, 1795; Rich-
        mond, 1799.

        BM CtY ICN NcD   1795: DLC MH NN
        1799: CSmH

774   Mercier de la Rivière, Pierre Paul François Joachim Henri, 1720–
        1793.
        L'Heureuse Nation, ou Relations du Gouvernement des Féli-
        ciens, Peuple Souverainement Libre sous l'Empire Absolu de
        Ses Loix. 2 vols. Paris, 1792.

        BM BN ICN MH

775   Mercurio Britannico (*pseud.*). *See* Hall, Joseph.

776   Meredith, Edgar.
        Our Stranger. A Kinemato-Romance. London, 1936. 407 p.

        BM NcD

777   Merezhkovskii, Dmitrii Sergieevich, 1865–1941.
        Das Irdische Paradise. Ein Märchen aus dem 27 Jahrhunderts.
        Eine Utopie. Translated by H. Mordaunt. Berlin, 1903.

        DLC NN

778   ————.
        The Secret of the West. Translated by John Cournos. New
        York, 1931. 449 p.

        CtY DLC NcD NN

779   Merrill, Albert Adams.
        The Great Awakening; the Story of the 22nd Century. Boston,
        1899. 345 p.

        CSmH CtY DLC MH NcD NN

780   Mette, John Allen, 1864–.
The Ideal State. Charleston, S.C., 1927. 58 p.

DLC MH

781   Meurville, Louis de.
La Cité Future. Paris, 1910. 325 p.

BM BN

782   Meyer, John Joseph.
Thirteen Seconds that Rocked the World, or, the Mentator. New York, 1935. 205 p.

DLC MH NcD NN

783   Meyern, Wilhelm Friedrich von, 1762–1829.
Dya-Na-Sore, oder die Wanderer. Vienna and Leipzig, 1787. 414 p.

BM   1789: CtY   1800: MH   1840: DLC
1886: ICU NcD

784   Michaelis, Richard C., 1839–1909.
Ein Blick in die Zukunft . . . eine Antwort auf Ein Rückblick, von Edward Bellamy. Chicago and New York, 1890. 173 p.

DLC MH

785   ————.
Looking Forward . . . An Answer to Looking Backward. Chicago, New York, and London, 1890. 123 p. (2nd edition titled: *Looking Further Forward.*)

BM CSmH CtY DLC ICN MH NcD NN

786   Michaud, Alfred Charles, 1876–.
Our Coming World. Philadelphia, 1951. 165 p.

CtY DLC MH NcD NN

787   Middleton, John B.
The God of This World. A Story for the Times. London, 1905. 205 p.

BM NcD

788   Miles (*pseud.*). *See* Southwold, Stephen.

789   Miller, Joaquin (Cincinnatus Heine Miller), 1841(?)–1913.
        The Building of the City Beautiful. Cambridge, Mass. and Chicago, 1893. 196 p.

        CSmH CtY DLC ICN ICU NcD   1894: BM   1905: NN

790   Miller, Walter M.
        A Canticle for Leibowitz. London, 1960. 320 p.

        BM MH NN   1961 (French): BN

791   Minnett, Cora.
        The Day after Tomorrow. London, 1911. 310 p.

        BM

792   [Misson, François Maximilien] (François Leguat), 1650(?)–1722.
        Voyage et Avantures de François Leguat et de Ses Compagnons en Deux Îsles Désertes des Indes Orientales. 2 vols. London, 1708. [Long accepted as the work of François Leguat. See Geoffroy Atkinson, "The Extraordinary Voyage," in *French Literature from 1700–1720* (New York, 1920), chap. 3.]

        BM BN CtY MH NcD NN   1721: DLC

793   [————].
        A New Voyage to the East-Indies by François Leguat and His Companions, Containing Their Adventures in Two Desert Islands. 2 vols. London, 1708.

        BM CSmH CtY ICN MH   1891: BN NcD

794   Mr. Dick (*pseud.*). *See* Dick, Mr.

795   Mitchell, James Leslie, 1901–1935.
        Gay Hunter. London, 1934. 286 p.

        BM NcD

796   Mitchell, John Ames, 1845–1918.
        The Last American, a Fragment from the Journal of Khon-li,

Prince of Dimph-Yoo-Chur and Admiral in the Persian Navy,
Edited by J. A. Mitchell. New York, 1889. 78 p.

BM CSmH CtY DLC ICU MH NcD NN

797   Mitchell, Willis.
The Inhabitants of Mars: Their Manners and Advancement in
Civilization and Their Opinion of Us. Malden, Mass., 1895.
178 p.

CSmH DLC

798   Moffat, W. Graham and John White.
What's the World Coming To? A Novel of the Twenty-First
Century. London, 1893. 172 p.

BM

799   Molinari, Gustave de, 1819–1912.
Esquisse de l'Organisation Politique et Économique de la So-
ciété Future. Paris, 1899. 242 p.

BM BN CtY DLC ICU MH NcD NN

800   ——————.
The Society of To-Morrow. Translated by P. H. Lee Warner.
New York and London, 1904. 230 p.

BM CtY DLC ICU MH NcD NN

801   Momoro, Antoine François, 1756–1794 (supposed author).
Histoire Intéressante d'un Nouveau Voyage à la Lune, et de la
Descente à Paris d'une Jolie Dame de Cette Terre Étrangère.
Paris, 1784. 92 p.

BN MH

802   Monro, Harold Edward. *See* Browne, Maurice.

803   Montenegro Baca, José.
Indoamerica en el Año 3850. Trujillo, Peru, 1941. 216 p.

DLC MH

804   Moore, Anon *(pseud.)*. *See* Galloway, James M.

805 Moore, David Albert, 1814–.
"The Age of Progress; or, a Panorama of Time." In *Four Visions*. New York, 1856. 321 p.

DLC ICN ICU MH

806 Moore, M. Louise.
Al-Modad; or, Life Scenes Beyond the Polar Circumflex. Shell Bank, La., 1892. 220 p.

DLC

807 Morata, Jaido (*pseud.*). *See* Vickers, John.

808 More, Sir Thomas, 1478–1535.
Libellus Vere Aureus Nec Minus Salutaris Quam Festivus de Optimo Reip. Statu, Deque Nova Insula Utopia. Louvain, 1516. 91 p.

BM BN Bod CSmH CtY DLC MH   1518: NN
1613: NcD

[The first English edition was a translation by Ralphe Robynson published in London, 1551.]

809 [Moreau, Jacob Nicolas], 1717–1804.
Nouveau Mémoire pour Servir à l'Histoire des Cacouacs. Amsterdam, 1757. 108 p.

BM BN CtY ICU MH NcD

810 [Morelly, abbé.]
*Naufrage des Îsles Flottantes, ou Basiliade du Célèbre Pilpai, Poeme Héroique Traduit de l'Indien par Mr. *******. 2 vols. Messine (i.e., Paris), 1753.

BN Bod DLC ICN ICU MH NcD NN

811 [————.]
The Basiliade: or, the Book of Truth and Nature. 2 vols. London, 1761.

DLC

812   Moresby, Charles, Lord.
       A Hundred Years Hence; or the Memoirs of Charles, Lord Moresby, Written by Himself. London, 1828. 210 p.
       BM

813   Morgan, Harriet.
       The Island Impossible. Boston, 1899. 206 p.
       DLC MH NcD

814   [Morgan, John Minter], 1782–1854.
       The Revolt of the Bees. London, 1826. 272 p.
       BM DLC ICN MH   1839: CtY ICU NcD NN

815   [————].
       "The Arrival in London of Vela, a Peruvian Missionary, from a Community of the Children of the Sun, Settled in the Most Inaccessible Part of South America Since the Expulsion by Pizarro.—Vela's History of the Community." In *Hampden in the Nineteenth Century,* chap. 14. London, 1834.
       BM CtY DLC ICN ICU NcD

816   Morgan, Joseph, 1671(?)–*ca.*1745 (probable author).
       The History of the Kingdom of Basaruah . . . By a Traveller in Basaruah. Boston, 1715. 160 p.
       CSmH MH

817   ————.
       The History of the Kingdom of Basaruah. . . . Edited by Richard Schlatter. Cambridge, Mass., 1946. 172 p.
       BM BN CtY DLC ICN ICU MH NcD NN

818   Morley, Felix, 1894–.
       Gumption Island. Caldwell, Idaho, 1956. 306 p.
       CtY DLC ICU NcD NN

819   [Morris, Alfred.]
       Looking Ahead. A Tale of Adventure. Not by the Author of "Looking Backward." London, 1891. 264 p.
       CtY MH   1892: BM

820   Morris, Mrs. Martha (Marlowe), 1867–, and Laura B. Speers.
       No Borderland. Dallas, Tex., 1938. 269 p.

       DLC NcD

821   Morris, William, 1834–1896.
       The Earthly Paradise. 3 vols. London, 1868.

       BM CSmH CtY DLC ICN ICU MH NcD NN
       1896: BN

822   ————.
       A Dream of John Ball. London, 1888. 141 p. [Published in
       Commonweal, 1886–87.]

       BM CSmH CtY ICN ICU MH NcD NN   1892: DLC
       Works: BN

823   ————.
       *News from Nowhere: or, an Epoch of Rest. Being Some Chap-
       ters from a Utopian Romance*. Boston, 1890; London, 1891.
       278 p. [Published in *Commonweal*, 1890.]

       BM CSmH DLC ICN MH NcD NN   1891: CtY ICU
       Works: BN

824   Moszkowski, Alexander, 1851–1934.
       The Isles of Wisdom. Translated by H. J. Stenning. New York
       and London, 1924. 322 p.

       BM DLC   1925: CtY NcD NN

825   Mouhy, Charles de Fieux, chevalier de (*pseud*. Fieux), 1701–1784.
       *Lamekis; ou, les Voyages Extraordinaires d'un Égyptien dans
       la Terre Intérieure Avec la Découverte de l'Île des Silphides*.
       2 vols. Paris, 1735–38.

       BN CtY ICN   1737: BM ICU   1787: CSmH DLC

826   Müller, Ernst.
       *Ein Rückblick aus dem Jahre 2037 auf das Jahr 2000 Aus den
       Erinnerungen des Herrn Julian West*. Berlin, 1891.

       ICN MH

827 ——————.
My Afterdream. London, 1900. 247 p.

BM MH

828 Müller, Walter.
Wenn Wir 1918 . . . eine Real-Politische Utopie. Berlin, 1930. 455 p.

DLC MH NN

829 Muggleton, Lodowick. *See* Reeve, John.

830 Mummery. *See* Lockhart-Mummery, John Percy.

831 Mundus, Jakob (*pseud.*). *See* Vetsch, Jakob.

832 N., T.
A Pleasant Dialogue Between a Lady Called Listra, and a Pilgrim. Concerning the Government and Common Weale of the Great Province of Crangalor. London, 1579.

Bod CSmH

833 ——————.
The Second Part of the Painefull Journey of the Poore Pilgrim into Asia, and the Straynge Wonders That He Sawe. London, 1579.

Bod CSmH

834 Nadal, Augustin, abbé, 1664–1740.
Les Voyages de Zulma dans le Pays des Fées. Amsterdam, 1734. 287 p.

BN DLC ICU NcD   1735: NN   1785: ICN

835 Navarchus (*pseud.*).
The World's Awakening. London, 1908. 463 p.

BM MH

836 Neck, J. Vander (*pseud.*). *See* Burgh, James.

837   Nedram (*pseud.*).
      John Sagur. London, 1921. 272 p.
      BM

838   Netterville, Luke (*pseud.*). *See* O'Grady, Standish James.

839   [Neville, Henry], 1620–1694.
      The Isle of Pines, or a Late Discovery of a Fourth Island, in Terra Australis Incognita . . . in a Letter from Cornelius van Sloetton. London, 1668. 31 p.
      BM CSmH CtY DLC ICN MH

840   [————].
      Plato Redivivus: or a Dialogue Concerning Government, Wherein, by Observations Drawn from Other Kingdoms and States Both Ancient and Modern, an Endeavor is Used to Discover the Present Politick Distemper of Our Own, With the Causes, and Remedies. London, 1681. 271 p.
      BM CSmH CtY DLC ICN MH NcD   1763: ICU

841   *The New Atlantis: or Ideals Old and New.* London, 1884. 208 p.
      BM DLC

842   *A New Discoverie of an Old Traveller Lately Arrived from Port-Dul, Shewing the Manner of the Country, Fashions of the People and Their Laws.* London, 1676. 6 p.
      CtY

843   Newcastle, Margaret (Lucas) Cavendish, duchess of, 1624–1674.
      The Inventory of Judgment's Commonwealth, Which the Author Cares Not in What World It Is Established. (Part III of *The World's Olio.*) London, 1655. 216 p.
      BM

844   ————.
      Observations upon Experimental Philosophy. To Which is Added the Description of a New Blazing World. London, 1666. 158 p.
      BM CtY MH   1668: ICN ICU

845   Newte, Horace Wykeham Can, 1870–1949.
The Master Beast: being a True Account of the Ruthless Tyranny Inflicted on the British People by Socialism, A.D. 1888–2020. London, 1907. 249 p.

BM DLC ICN NcD NN

846   Niau, Josephine Hyacinthe.
The Phantom Paradise. The Story of the Expedition of the Marquis de Rays. Sydney, 1936. 189 p.

BM CtY NN

847   Niemann, August (Wilhelm Otto August), 1839–1919.
The Coming Conquest of England. Translated by J. H. Freeze. London, 1904. 384 p.

BM DLC MH NcD NN

848   [Nimes, Joseph A.]
Aristocracy. A Novel. New York, 1888. 257 p.

BM DLC NcD NN

849   *Nineteen Hundred and Seventy-Five: a Tradition.* London, 1875.

Bod

850   Noland. *See* Free State of Noland.

851   Norelli, Peter.
Utop Anno 2000 Wertumwertung, Bericht über die Erste Tagung des Internationalen Intersäkularen Weltverbandes der Utopisten (10–17 Juni 2000). Vienna, 1936. 182 p.

NcD

852   Nork, F. (*pseud.*). *See* Korn, Friedrich.

853   Nostradamus, Merlin (*pseud.*). *See* Cobbe, Francis Power.

854   Noto, Cosimo, M.D.
The Ideal City. New York, 1903. 377 p.

CtY DLC ICN ICU NcD NN

855   Nott, Kathleen.
        The Dry Deluge. London, 1947. 307 p.
        BM NN

856   O'Duffy, Eimar Ultan, 1893–1935.
        King Goshawk and the Birds. London, 1926. 318 p.
        BM CtY DLC ICU MH NcD NN

857   ————.
        The Spacious Adventures of the Man in the Street. London,
        1928. 406 p.
        BM DLC NcD NN

858   ————.
        Asses in Clover. London and New York, 1933. 331 p.
        BM DLC NcD NN

859   [O'Grady, Standish James] (*pseud.* Luke Netterville), 1846–1923.
        The Queen of the World; or, Under the Tyranny. London,
        1900. 293 p.
        BM CSmH CtY ICU

860   Olerich, Henry, 1851–.
        A Cityless and Countryless World. Holstein, Iowa, 1893. 447 p.
        CSmH DLC ICN ICU MH NcD NN

861   ————.
        *Modern Paradise; an Outline or Story of How Some of the
        Cultured People Will Probably Live, Work, and Organize in
        the New Future.* Omaha, Neb., 1915. 198 p.
        DLC CtY NcD

862   ————.
        The Story of the World a Thousand Years Hence. Omaha,
        Neb., 1923. 117 p.
        DLC ICN MH NcD NN

863   Oliver, Daniel.
      *The Foreign Visitant: Containing Interesting Observations and
      Remarks Made by an Inhabitant of Terra Incognita, on the
      Character and Manners of the Inhabitants of This Earth.* Bos-
      ton, 1814. 17 p.

      CtY

864   Oliver, George (*pseud*. Oliver Onions).
      The New Moon: a Romance of Reconstruction. London, 1918.
      312 p.

      BM DLC MH

865   Olivera, Roberto Miguel.
      Se Acaba el Mundo; o, el Libro de Proscopio. Novela. Monte-
      video, 1943. 238 p.

      CtY DLC NcD NN

866   Ollivant, Alfred, 1874–.
      Tomorrow; a Romance of the Future. London, 1927. 320 p.

      BM DLC ICN MH NcD NN

867   O'Neil, Henry, 1817–1880.
      Two Thousand Years Hence. London, 1868. 351 p.

      BM MH

868   Onions, Oliver (*pseud*.). *See* Oliver, George.

869   Ophirischer Staat. *See* Der Wohleingerichtete Staat.

870   Orpen, Adela Elizabeth Richards.
      Perfection City. New York. 1897. 310 p.

      BM CSmH DLC NcD NN

871   Orwell, George (*pseud*.). *See* Blair, Eric Arthur.

872   *Our Sister Republic, a Single Tax Story.* New York, 1911. 54 p.

      DLC NN

873   [Ouseley, Gideon Jasper Richard.]
       Palingenesia: or, the Earth's New Birth. By Theosopho, a
       Minister of the Holies, and Ellora, a Seeress of the Sanctuary.
       Glasgow, 1884. 359 p.

       BM MH

874   Owen, Albert Kimsey.
       A Dream of an Ideal City. London, 1897. 15 p.

       CSmH DLC

875   Pain, Barry Eric Odell, 1864–1928.
       The New Gulliver and Other Stories. London, 1912. 261 p.

       BM ICU NcD

876   ————.
       Futurist Fifteen. An Old Moore or Less Accurate Forecast of
       Certain Events in the Year 1915. London, 1914. 115 p.

       BM NN

877   [Palafox y Mendoza, Juan de], bishop of Osma, 1600–1659 (possible
       author).
       Relation du Voyage Mystérieux de l'Île de la Vertu, à Oronte.
       Paris, 1696. 128 p.

       BN ICN   1711: CtY DLC

878   [————].
       Relation du Voyage Mystérieux. . . . Edited by J. T. Hérissant
       and Louis Théodore Hérissant. Paris, 1760. 99 p.

       BM BN MH   1819: NcD

879   [Palissot de Montenoy, Charles], 1730–1814.
       Apollon Mentor, ou le Télémaque Moderne. 2 vols. in 1. Lon-
       don, 1748.

       BM BN NcD

880 Pallander, Edwin.
Across the Zodiac. A Story of Adventure. London, 1896. 306 p.

BM MH NcD

881 Pallen, Condé Benoist, 1858–1929.
Crucible Island. A Romance, an Adventure and an Experiment.
New York, 1919. 215 p.

CtY DLC ICN NcD NN   1920: BM

882 Palmer, Frederick, 1873–.
So a Leader Came. New York, 1932. 367 p.

BM CtY DLC ICN MH NcD NN

883 Palmer, John Leslie, 1885–1944.
The Hesperides. A Looking-Glass Fugue. London, 1936. 318 p.

BM NcD

884 [Paltock, Robert], 1697–1767.
*The Life and Adventures of Peter Wilkins, a Cornish Man,
Relating . . . His Wonderful Passage Thro' a Subterraneous
Cavern into a Kind of New World . . . a Description of This
Same Country, With the Laws, Customs, and Manners of Its
Inhabitants.* 2 vols. London, 1751.

BM CSmH CtY MH NcD   1783: DLC NN
1784: ICN   1847: ICU

885 [————].
The Life and Adventures of Peter Wilkins. . . . New York,
1915. 352 p.

BM BN Bod CSmH CtY DLC ICN ICU MH NcD NN

886 Pan (*pseud.*). *See* Beresford, Leslie.

887 Papp, Desiderius, 1895–.
Creation's Doom. Translated by H. J. Stenning. London, 1934.
287 p.

BM CtY DLC NcD NN

888 Paraf, Pierre, 1893–.
    Les Cités du Bonheur. Paris, 1945. 277 p.
    BM BN DLC ICU MH NN

889 Parazols, Denis.
    Rêve à Vénus. Anticipation Sociale. Marseilles, 1935. 293 p.
    NcD

890 Parker, Joseph W.
    Doctor Crosby's Strange Experience; or, a New World by 1944.
    Kansas City, Mo., 1935. 90 p.
    DLC NcD

891 Parry, David Maclean, 1852–1915.
    The Scarlet Empire. Indianapolis, 1906. 400 p.
    BM CtY DLC MH NcD NN

892 *Pasquin Risen from the Dead; or, His Own Relations of a Late
    Voyage He Made to the Other World.* London, 1674. 245 p.
    Bod CtY DLC ICU

893 [Paton, J.] (probable author).
    Balmanno: the City of Our Quest and Its Social Problems.
    Paisley, Scotland, 1906. 233 p.
    BM

894 Patrizzi, Francesco, da Cherso (Patritio), 1529–1597.
    La Città Felice. Venice, 1553. 69 ff.
    BM BN ICN

895 ————.
    Utopisti e Riformatori Sociali del Quinquecento. Bologna, 1941.
    NN

896 Pauer, Louis.
    *Eurekanian Paternalism; for an Economic Expedition to Ex-
    plore and Exploit Eurekania, the New State in the Realm of
    Utopia.* Cleveland, 1923. 26 p.
    CtY DLC MH NN

897   Pawlowski, Gaston William Adam de, 1874–1933.
         Voyage au Pays de la Quatrième Dimension. Paris, 1912. 324 p.

         BM BN NcD

898   Pechméja, Jean de, 1741–1785.
         Télephe. London and Paris, 1784. 264 p.

         BM BN NN   1795: MH

899   Peck, Bradford.
         *The World a Department Store: a Story of Life Under a
         Coöperative System.* Lewiston, Me., and Boston, 1900. 311 p.

         BM CSmH CtY DLC ICN ICU MH NcD NN

900   Péguy, Charles Pierre, 1873–1914.
         Marcel; Premier Dialogue de la Cité Harmonieuse. Paris, 1898.
         240 p.

         BN   1932: BM CtY   1933: MH NN   1973: NcD

901   Pemberton, Robert.
         The Happy Colony. London, 1854. 217 p.

         BM BN DLC MH NN

902   Perce, Elbert, 1831–1869.
         *Gulliver Joi: His Three Voyages; Being an Account of His
         Marvelous Adventures in Kailoo, Hydrogenia and Ejario.* New
         York, 1851. 272 p.

         CtY DLC ICU   1852: NcD NN

903   Pernal, Francisco V.
         La Biblia del Pernalismo. Cervera, 1933. 476 p.

         DLC

904   Pernetti, Jacques, 1696–1777.
         *Le Repos de Cyrus, ou l'Histoire de Sa Vie, Depuis Sa Seizième
         Jusqu'à Sa Quarantième Année.* 3 vols. Paris, 1732.

         BM BN DLC MH NcD NN

905   Perry, James Raymond.
       "The Constitution of Carnegia." *North American Review* 175
       (1902): 243–53.
       BM BN CtY DLC ICN ICU MH NcD NN

906   Perry, Walter Copland, 1814–1911.
       The Revolt of the Horses. London, 1898. 229 p.
       BM NcD

907   Perrycoste. *See* Coste, Frank Hill Perry.

908   Persinger, Charles Edward.
       *Letters from New America; or, an Attempt at Practical So-
       cialism.* Chicago, 1900. 89 p.
       NN

909   [Petersilea, Carlyle] (*pseud.* Ernest von Himmel), 1844–1903.
       The Discovered Country. Boston, 1889. 234 p.
       MH NN   1892: NcD

910   Peterson, Ephraim.
       An Ideal City for an Ideal People. Independence, Mo., 1905.
       134 p.
       DLC ICN MH

911   ————.
       Redemption. Independence, Mo., 1909. 140 p.
       DLC NN

912   [Petit de Brétigny, Jonathas] (Bertigny).
       L'Anti Hermaphrodite, ou le Secret. Paris, 1606. 669 p.
       BM BN ICN ICU

913   Petrus Firmianus. *See* Zacherie de Lisieux.

914   Petworth, Algernon.
       The Little Wicket Gate . . . An Experience ex Nihilo. London,
       1913. 252 p.
       BM

915   Petzler, J. Aloys.
> *Die Sociale Baukunst; oder, Gründe und Mittel für den Um-*
> *sturz und Wiederaufbau der Gesellschaftlichen Verhältnisse,*
> *Besonders wie Solche Sich in Neuester Zeit in England, dem*
> *Grossen Musterstaat der Modernen Civilisation, Ausgebildet*
> *Haben.* 2 vols. Zurich, 1879–80.

MH NN

916   Petzler, Johann.
> *Life in Utopia.* London, 1890. 183 p.

BM NcD

917   Pezet, Alfonso Washington, 1889–.
> *Aristokia.* New York, 1919. 214 p.

BM CtY DLC ICN MH NcD

918   [Pfeiffer, Johann Gregor] (Grazianus Agricola Auletes).
> *Graziani Agricolae Auletis Sonderbahre Reisen in Unbekandte*
> *Länder. Aus Richtig Gehaltenen Diariis, Auffgezeichneten*
> *Anmerckungen, und Angmerckten Entdeckungen. Gedruckt*
> *zu Hanochia, in der Ophirischen Landschafft Canaan.* Bremen
> (?), 1721–22. 947 p.

BM

919   Phelon, William P.
> *Our Story of Atlantis. Written Down for the Hermetic Broth-*
> *erhood and the Future Rulers of America.* San Francisco, 1903.
> 217 p.

CtY DLC NcD   1937: NN

920   [Phelps, George Hamilton] (*pseud.* Patrick Quinn Tangent), 1854–.
> *The New Columbia; or, The Re-United States.* Findlay, Ohio,
> 1909. 99 p.

DLC ICU MH NN

921   "A Pilgrimage to Utopia; or the Autobiography of a Visionary."
> *Eclectic Review* 91 (March-April 1850): 353–62, 470–77.

BM DLC ICN ICU MH NN

922 [Pirret, Corsar.]
Queen Flora's Recollections; Being a True Synthetic Record of the Events Immediately Preceding the Glorious Restoration of the Monarchy in the Year of our Lord, 1998. London, 1911.
MH

923 Pocock, Roger.
The Chariot of the Sun. London, 1910. 305 p.
BM NcD

924 Poisson, Ernest, 1882–.
La République Coopérative. Paris, 1920. 256 p.
BM BN DLC NN

925 ———.
The Co-operative Republic. Translated by W. P. Watkins. London, 1925. 226 p.
BM CtY DLC NcD NN

926 Posnack, Emanuel Robert, 1897–.
The 21st Century Sizes Us Up. New York, 1942. 79 p.
CtY DLC NN

927 ———.
The 21st Century Looks Back. New York, 1946. 241 p.
DLC MH NcD NN

928 Postel, Guillaume, 1510–1581.
De Orbis Terrae Concordia. Basle, 1544. 427 p.
BM BN DLC ICN MH NN

929 *Posterity, Its Verdicts and its Methods; or, Democracy A.D. 2100.* London, 1897. 171 p.
BM ICU MH NN

930 *Premiére Relation du Voyage Fait Dans la Lune.* 3 vols. in 1. Paris (?), 1751.
NcD

931   Pressey, Edward Pearson, 1869–.
> *The Vision of New Clairvaux; or Ethical Reconstruction Through Combination of Agriculture and Handicraft.* Boston, 1909. 217 p.

    NN

932   Prevel, Louis.
> *L'Heure de la République Intégrale; par le Machine Automatique, Tout Produire pour tout Distribuer à Tout le Monde, Sans Rien Prendre à Personne.* Paris, 1945. 39 p.

    BN CtY DLC NN

933   [Prévost, Antoine François (Prévost d'Exiles)], 1697–1763.
> *Le Philosophe Anglois, ou Histoire de Monsieur Cleveland, Fils Naturel de Cromwel.* 8 vols. Paris, 1731.

    BN   1744: Bod DLC NcD   1777: BM CtY MH

934   ———.
> *The Life and Entertaining Adventures of Mr. Cleveland, Natural Son of Oliver Cromwell, Written by Himself.* 2 vols. London, 1732.

    ICU NN   1734: BM Bod CSmH CtY ICN
    1736: NcD   1741: DLC

935   *Private Letters of an American in England to His Friends in America.* London, 1769. 163 p.

    CtY DLC

936   ———.
> *Anticipation; or, the Voyage of an American to England in the Year 1889, in a Series of Letters, Humorously Describing the Supposed Situation of This Kingdom at That Period.* London, 1781. 163 p.

    BM Bod CtY ICN MH NcD NN

937   Pruning Knife (*pseud.*). *See* Allen, Henry Francis.

938   Puaux, René, 1878–1937.
> *La Grande Vague.* Paris, 1925. 222 p.

    BN DLC

939   Purchas, Samuel, *d. ca.* 1658.
    A Theatre of Politicall Flying-Insects, Wherein Especially the Nature, the Worth, the Work, the Wonder, and the Manner of Right-Ordering of the Bee, Is Discovered and Described . . . And in the Second Part Are Annexed Meditations and Observations Theological and Moral. London, 1657. 387 p.

    BM BN CSmH CtY DLC ICN ICU MH NcD NN

940   Quantin, Albert, 1850–.
    En Plein Vol, Vision d'Avenir. Paris, 1913. 313 p.
    BM BN

941   R., M. *See* Raguet, Gilles Bernard.

942   Rademacher, Hanna (Leuchs), 1881–.
    Utopia; ein Heiteres Spiel in Drei Aufzügen. Dresden and Düsseldorf, 1920. 71 p.

    CtY MH NN

943   Radical Freelance (*pseud.*).
    The Philosophers of Foufouville. New York, 1868. 297 p.

    BM CSmH DLC MH NcD NN

944   [Raguet, Gilles Bernard, abbé], 1668–1748.
    La Nouvelle Atlantide Continuée Avec des Réflexions sur l'Institution et les Occupations des Académies Française, des Sciences et des Inscriptions. Paris, 1702. 253 p.

    BM BN CtY

945   de Ramsay, chevalier Andrew Michael, 1686–1743.
    Les Voyages de Cyrus, Avec un Discours sur la Mythologie. 2 vols. Paris, 1727.

    BM BN MH   1728: ICU   1730: CSmH
    1753: CtY   1796: NN   1807: DLC

946   ———.

The Travels of Cyrus. To Which is Annexed, a Discourse Upon the Theology & Mythology of the Ancients. 2 vols. London, 1727.

BM CtY ICN ICU   1728: BN NcD   1730: DLC MH
1793: CSmH NN

947   ———.

A Criticism Upon Mr. Ramsay's Travels of Cyrus: Wherein the Character of Cyrus is Clear'd Up. By [*Stephen Whatley*]. London, 1729. 219 p.

NcD

948   Ramsey, Percival (*pseud.* Ramsey Benson).
A Lord of Lands. New York, 1908. 326 p.

CtY DLC MH NcD

949   Raphael, Mother Frances. *See* Drane, Augusta Theodosia.

950   Rationalis (*pseud.*).
"Remarks Which Are Supposed Will Be Made in This Kingdom, By Two North American Travelers in the Year One Thousand Nine Hundred and Forty-Four." In *The Literary Register; or, Weekly Miscellany* (London, 1769–73) 1:98–99.

BM CtY NcD

951   Reeve, John, 1608–1658, and Lodowick Muggleton, 1609–1698.
A Divine Looking Glass; or, the Third and Last Testament of Our Lord Jesus Christ. London, 1656. 208 p.

1661: BM CSmH MH   1719: CtY   1760: NcD NN

952   Regnas, C.
The Land of Nison. London, 1906. 319 p.

BM

953   Régnier, Yves.
Le Royaume de Bénou. Paris, 1957. 215 p.

BN CtY DLC MH

954 Reichardt, Alexander, 1858–1922.
Des Bellamy Zeitalter, 2001–2010. Erfindungen, Entdeckungen und Begebnisse. Berlin, 1893. 175 p.

ICN

955 Reinser III (*pseud.*). *See* Resnier, André Guillaume.

956 Reitmeister, Louis Aaron, 1903–.
If Tomorrow Comes. New York, 1934. 348 p.

CtY DLC NcD NN

957 Renouvier, Charles Bernard Joseph, 1815–1903.
Uchronie. (L'Utopie dans l'Histoire). Esquisse Historique Apocryphe du Développement de la Civilisation Européenne tel Qu'il n'a pas Été, Tel Qu'il Aurait pu Être. Paris, 1876. 413 p.

BM BN ICU NN   1901: CtY MH NcD

958 [Resnier, André Guillaume] (*pseud.* Reinser III), 1729–1811.
République Universelle, ou, l'Humanité Ailée, Réunie Sous l'Empire de la Raison. Geneva (?), 1788. 398 p.

BN DLC

959 [Restif de la Bretonne, Nicolas Edme], 1734–1806.
La Découverte Australe par un Homme Volant, ou le Dédale Français. 4 vols. Paris, 1781.

BN CSmH CtY DLC ICN MH NN

960 Restrepo, Roberto.
Discarquismo; o, Si la Razon Fuera Gobierno. Manizales, Colombia, 1936. 209 p.

DLC MH NN   1951: NcD

961 *The Rev. John Smith Died—and Went to Jupiter Via Hell.* New York, 1908. 318 p.

NN

962   Reybaud, Louis, 1799–1879.
        Jérome Paturot à la Recherche d'une Position Sociale. 2 vols.
        Paris, 1842.

        BM BN   1844: MH NN   1846: CtY DLC ICN
        1847: ICU NcD

963   Reynaert, John Hugh, 1843–.
        *The Eldorado of Socialism. Communism and Anarchism; or,
        a Trip to the Planet Jupiter.* Orlando, Fla., 1917. 86 p.

        DLC ICN MH

964   Reynolds, James. *See* Equality.

965   Reynolds, P. E.
        *Étude Sur le Monde Politique de la Troisième République. Aux
        Lueurs du "Grand Soir," Vers la Cité Socialiste, Roman d'Au-
        jourd'Hui et de Demain.* Paris, 1908. 369 p.

        BN

966   Rice, Elmer L., 1892–.
        A Voyage to Purilia. New York, 1930. 297 p.

        BM CtY DLC MH NcD NN   1934 (French): BN

967   Rice, James. *See* Besant, Sir Walter.

968   Rich, Barnaby, 1540(?)–1617.
        *A Right Excelent and Pleasant Dialogue, Betwene Mercury and
        an English Souldier: Contayning His Supplication to Mars:
        Beutified With Sundry Other Histories, Rare Inventions, and
        Politike Devises.* London, 1574. (No pagination.)

        BM

969   Richards, Charles Napier.
        Atlanta; or, Twelve Months in the Evening Star. Brighton,
        1909. 271 p.

        BM NcD

970   Richardson, E.
       Neutopia. London, 1925. 304 p.

       BM NcD

971   Richardson, Jasper (*pseud.*).
       *A True and Faithful Account of the Island of Veritas. . . . As
       Delivered in Several Sermons Just Published in Veritas.* [Edited
       by Nilekaw Freeman.] London, 1790(?). 171 p.

       BM CtY MH NN

972   Richter, Eugen, 1838–1906.
       Sozialdemokratische Zukunftsbilder. Berlin, 1891. 48 p.

       BN CtY   1892: DLC MH NN   1898: BM

973   ————.
       Pictures of the Socialistic Future. Translated by Henry Wright.
       London, 1893. 134 p.

       BM ICN ICU NN   1894: DLC   1912: MH NcD
       1925: CtY

974   Rico.
       *El Año Mil Novecientos y Tantos, la Conflagración Sudameri-
       cana.* La Paz, Bolivia, 1925. 172 p.

       DLC ICU

975   Ridley, Francis Ambrose.
       The Green Machine. London, 1926. 255 p.

       BM NcD

976   Rizk, C. M.
       The Paradise City. Philadelphia, 1933. 22 p.

       NN

977   Roberti, Giovanni Battista, 1719–1786.
       La Moda. Poemetto. Venice, 1746. 47 p.

       CtY DLC NcD   1797: BM

978 Roberts, J. W.
Looking Within. The Misleading Tendencies of "Looking Backward" Made Manifest. New York, 1893. 279 p.

BM CSmH CtY DLC ICN ICU MH NcD NN

979 Robertson (*pseud.*).
Voyage de Robertson aux Terres Australes, Traduit sur le Manuscrit Anglais. Amsterdam, 1766. 474 p.

BM BN CtY ICU NcD NN

980 [Röcken, Kurt Walter] (*pseud.* Henry Walter), 1906–.
Der Ruf vom Mond; Utopischer Roman. Linz, 1947. 320 p.

DLC NN

981 [Roe, William James] (*pseud.* Hudor Genone), 1843–.
Inquirendo Island. New York and London, 1886. 347 p.

BM CSmH CtY DLC   1890: NcD

982 [Rolfe, Frederick William Serafino Austin Lewis Mary] (*pseud.* Baron Frederick Corvo), 1860–1913.
Hadrian the Seventh. A Romance. London, 1904. 413 p.

BM CtY ICN MH   1925: DLC NcD   1937: ICU NN
1950: BN

983 Rosewater, Frank, 1856–.
'96; a Romance of Utopia. Omaha, Neb., 1894. 268 p.

BM CtY DLC ICN   1897: NcD

984 ————.
The Making of a Millenium. Omaha, Neb., 1908. 183 p.

BM CtY ICU NN

985 ————.
Doomed . . . an Antediluvian Romance of Two Old Worlds. New York, 1920. 282 p.

DLC NcD NN

986   Rousseau, Victor (*pseud.*). *See* Emmanuel, Victor Rousseau.

987   Russell, Addison Peale, 1826–1912.
       Sub-Coelum; a Sky-Built Human World. Boston and New York, 1893. 267 p.

       BM CSmH CtY DLC ICN ICU MH NcD NN

988   [Russell, John Russell, earl] (attributed author), 1792–1878.
       Adventures in the Moon, and Other Worlds. London, 1836. 447 p.

       BM DLC NcD

989   Russell, T. Baron.
       A Hundred Years Hence. The Expectations of an Optimist. London, 1905. 312 p.

       BM CtY ICN   1906: NcD NN

990   [Rustaing de Saint-Jory, Louis] *d.* 1752.
       Les Femmes Militaires, Relation Historique d'une Île Nouvellement Découverte . . . par le C. D. ***. Paris, 1735. 316 p.

       BN DLC   1736: Bod MH   1739: CtY NN

991   [Sade, Donatien Alphonse François, comte (called marquis de)], 1740–1814.
       Aline et Valcour, ou le Roman Philosophique; Écrit à la Bastille. 7 vols. Paris, 1795.

       BN   1883: CtY DLC   1956: ICU MH   1962: NcD

992   Sadeur, Jacques (*pseud.*). *See* Foigny, Gabriel de.

993   Salisbury, Henry Barnard.
       The Birth of Freedom. New York, 1890. 149 p.
       [First published in the *Nationalist Magazine,* 1890; republished in *Brotherhood of London;* published in book form as *Miss Worden's Hero;* original title resumed in 3d edition.]

       1894: DLC NN

994   Salisbury, William, 1875–.
The American Emperor. New York, 1913. 398 p.
DLC NcD NN

995   ————.
The Squareheads, the Story of a Socialized State, a Futuristic Novel. New Rochelle, N.Y., 1929. 168 p.
CtY NcD NN

996   Samuel, Herbert Louis Samuel, viscount, 1870–.
An Unknown Land. London, 1942. 221 p.
BM CtY DLC MH NcD NN

997   [Samuels, Philip Francis] (*pseud.* Samuels Bacon), 1881–.
Bensalem and New Jerusalem. Boston, 1936. 154 p.
BM DLC MH NcD

998   San Blas, Caesario, Bachelor (*pseud.*).
A Voyage to the Island of Philosophers, Containing an Account of the Island and Its Inhabitants. New York (?), 1830. 53 p.
University of Illinois, Urbana, Ill.

999   Sarban (*pseud.*). *See* Wall, John W.

1000   Saunders, W. J.
Kalomera: the Story of a Remarkable Community. London, 1911. 301 p.
BM DLC NN

1001   Savage, Timothy (*pseud.?*).
The Amazonian Republic, Recently Discovered in the Interior of Peru. New York, 1842. 177 p.
BM CtY DLC ICN ICU MH NN

1002   Say, Jean Baptiste, 1767–1832.
Olbie; ou Essai Sur les Moyens de Réformer les Moeurs d'une Nation. Paris, 1800. 132 p.
BM BN ICU MH NcD   1848: DLC ICN

1003   Sceriman, Zacharias. *See* Seriman, Zaccaria.

1004   Schafheitlin, Adolf, 1852–1917.
        Der Grosse Ironiker und Sein Werk. Träumereien Zwischen Fels und Meer. 2 vols. Berlin, 1907–9.

        DLC ICU MH

1005   Schellhous, E. J.
        The New Republic: Founded on the Natural and Inalienable Rights of Man, and Containing the Outlines of Such a Government as the Patriot Fathers Contemplated and Formulated in the Declaration of Independence When Struggling for Liberty. San Francisco, 1883. 354 p.

        CSmH DLC ICN ICU NcD   1887: BM

1006   Schindler, Solomon, 1842–1915.
        Young West; a Sequel to Edward Bellamy's Celebrated Novel, Looking Backward. Boston, 1894. 283 p.

        CSmH CtY DLC ICN ICU MH NcD NN

1007   Schirmeister, Erich, 1880–.
        Marlo-Winkelblech und Sein Zukunftsstaat. Greifswald, 1904. 46 p.

        DLC MH NN

1008   Schleyer, Johann Martin, 1831–1912.
        Ein Idealvolk. Vision. Constance, 1912. 24 p.

        NN

1009   [Schmidt, Willy] (*pseud.* German Gerhold), 1896–.
        Das Letzte Gesetz, der Durchbruch zum Weltbild der Kommenden Epoche. Stuttgart, 1946. 402.

        DLC NN

1010   [Schnabel, Johann Gottfried] (*pseud.* Eberhard Julius Gisander), 1692–1750.
        Wunderliche Fata einiger See-Fahrer . . . auch par Commission dem Drucke Übergeben von Gisandern. Nordhausen, 1731.

608 p. [4 volumes issued successively with different titles; the work became generally known as *Die Insel Felsenburg*.]

BM   1736: CtY MH   1737: DLC ICU

1011   [————].
Die Insel Felsenburg. Edited by Hermann Ullrich. Berlin, 1902. 468 p.

BM BN CtY DLC ICN ICU MH NcD NN

1012   [Schnebelin, ————.]
Erklärung der Wunder-Seltsamen Land-Charten Utopiae, so Da Ist, das Neu-Entdeckte Schlarraffenland. Arbeitshausen (Nuremberg?), *ca.* 1650. 396 p.

CtY   1730: BM MH

1013   Schooten, Hendrik (*pseud.?*).
The Hairy-Giants, or, a Description of Two Islands in the South Sea, Called by the Names of Benganga and Coma . . . Written in Dutch and Englished by P. M., Gent. London, 1671. 16 p.

BM BN DLC MH   1766: ICN

1014   Schuette, H. George, 1850–.
Athonia; or, the Original Four Hundred. Manitowoc, Wis., 1910. 483 p.

CtY DLC ICN MH NN   1911: NcD

1015   Schütz, von. *See* Sinold, Philipp Balthasar.

1016   [Scott, Mrs. Sarah (Robinson)], 1723–1795.
A Description of Millenium Hall, and the Country Adjacent. London, 1762. 262 p.

BM CSmH CtY ICN ICU MH NcD NN   1764: DLC

1017   [————].
A Description of Millenium Hall. . . . Edited by Walter M. Crittenden. New York, 1955. 200 p.

BM CSmH CtY DLC ICN MH NcD NN

1018   Scrymsour, Ella M.
The Perfect World, a Romance of Strong People and Strong Places. London, 1922. 320 p.
BM DLC MH NcD

1019   Seaborn, Capt. Adam (*pseud.*). (Attributed to John Cleves Symmes.)
Symzonia: a Voyage of Discovery. New York, 1820. 248 p.
BM CSmH CtY DLC ICN ICU

1020   ———.
Symzonia. . . . Edited by J. O. Bailey. Gainesville, Fla., 1965. 248 p.
DLC ICU MH NcD

1021   [Seriman, Zaccaria (Zacharias Sceriman)], 1708–1784.
Viaggi di Enrico Wanton alle Terre Incognite Australi, ed al Paese delle Scimmie. 2 vols. in 1. Venice, 1748–49.
CtY   1764: DLC ICN NcD NN   1769: BM
1772: ICU

1022   Serly, Ludovicus Textoris, 1855–.
Stop! . . . Distracted People! Two Mirrors of the Future; Romantic Double Utopia. New York, 1937. 163 p.
DLC NN

1023   Sgualdi, Vincenzo, 1580–1652.
Republica di Lesbo, Overo della Ragione di Stato in un Domino Aristocratico. Bologna, 1640. 376 p.
BN ICN   1643: BM

1024   Shanks, Edward, 1892–.
The People of the Ruins; a Story of the English Revolution and After. New York, 1920. 314 p.
BM CtY DLC MH NcD NN

1025   Shelley, Mrs. Mary Wollstonecraft (Godwin), 1797–1851.
The Last Man. 3 vols. London, 1826.
BM BN CSmH CtY DLC ICN ICU MH
1833: NcD NN

1026 ———————.
    The Last Man. Edited by Hugh J. Luke. Lincoln, Neb., 1965. 342 p.
    BM DLC ICU MH NcD

1027 Shelley, Percy Bysshe, 1792–1822.
    "The Assassins. A Fragment of a Romance." In *Essays, Letters from Abroad, Translations and Fragments,* edited by Mrs. Shelley, 1:182–211. London, 1840. (Probably written in 1816.)
    BM CtY DLC ICN MH NcD NN   1852: ICU

1028 Shiel, Matthew Phipps, 1865–1947.
    The Lord of the Sea. New York, 1901. 474 p.
    BM DLC NN   1924: CtY MH   1929: NcD

1029 ———————.
    The Purple Cloud. London, 1901. 463 p.
    BM NN   1929: CtY DLC MH   1930: ICN

1030 Short, Gertrude.
    A Visitor from Venus. New York, 1949. 43 p.
    DLC NcD NN

1031 Siano, Francesco de.
    La Città dell' Uomo. Turin, 1954. 133 p.
    NcD NN

1032 Sibbern, Frederick Christian, 1785–1872.
    Meddelelser af Indholdet af et Skrivt fra Aaret 2135. 2 vols. in 1. Copenhagen, 1858–72.
    BM MH NcD NN

1033 Sibthorpe, H. *See* Fox, Lady Mary.

1034 Siden, Captain (*pseud.*). *See* Vairasse, Denis.

1035 Sigurdsson, Ingvar, 1885–.
    Auf zum Weltreich! Aus dem Islandischen von Rudolf K. Kinsky. Vienna, 1934.
    Bod MH

1036   [Simpson, William] (*pseud.* Thomas Blot), 1828–1910.
       The Man from Mars, His Morals, Politics and Religion. San
       Francisco, 1891. 173 p.

       CSmH DLC MH NcD   1893: NN

1037   Singer, Ignatius. *See* Berens, Lewis Henry.

1038   [Sinold, Philipp Balthasar (von Schütz)] (*pseud.* Ludwig Ernst
       von Faramond), 1657–1742.
       *Die Glückseeligste Insul auf der Gantzen Welt, oder das Land
       der Zufriedenheit.* Königsberg, 1723. 340 p.

       BM ICU   1737: CtY   1749: MH

       [BM catalogues the 1723 edition under Wahrenburg, Constan-
       tinus von.]

1039   Skinner, Burrhus Frederic, 1904–.
       Walden Two. New York, 1948. 266 p.

       CtY DLC ICN ICU MH NcD NN   1960: BM

1040   Skorpios, Antares (*pseud.*). *See* Barlow, James William.

1041   Slater, Henry J.
       The Smashed World. London, 1952. 221 p.

       BM NcD

1042   Sloetton, Cornelius van. *See* Neville, Henry.

1043   Smart, Charles Allen, 1904–.
       Rosscommon. New York, 1940. 201 p.

       CtY DLC MH NcD NN

1044   Smeeks, Hendrick, *d.* 1721.
       Beschryvinge van het Magtig Koningryk Krinke Kesmes. Am-
       sterdam, 1708. 286 p.

       BM CtY ICN MH   1751: DLC   1776: BN

1045   ————.
       A Dutch Source for Robinson Crusoe; the Narrative of the

El-Ho "Sjouke Gabbes" (also known as Henrich Texel), an Episode from the Description of the Mighty Kingdom of Krinke Kesmes . . . Translated and Compared with the Story of Robinson Crusoe by Lucius L. Hubbard. Ann Arbor, Mich., 1921. 172 p.

BM CSmH CtY DLC ICN ICU MH NcD NN

1046   Smith, Titus Keiper, 1859–.
        Altruria. New York, *ca.* 1895. 120 p.

        BM CSmH CtY DLC ICN MH NcD NN

1047   [Smollett, Tobias George], 1721–1771.
        The History and Adventures of an Atom. 2 vols. London, 1769.
        [First issue has erroneous date 1749.]

        BM CtY DLC ICN ICU

1048   [————].
        "The History and Adventures of an Atom." In *Miscellaneous Works of Smollett,* 2:915–66. London, 1858.

        BM ICN ICU MH NcD NN

1049   Souëtre, Olivier, 1871–1930.
        La Cité de l'Égalité. Paris, 1896. 56 p.

        BM BN

1050   [Southwold, Stephen], (*pseuds.* Miles; Neill Bell), 1887–.
        The Seventh Bowl. London, 1930. 252 p.

        BM NcD

1051   Souvestre, Émile, 1806–1854.
        Le Monde Tel Qu'il Sera. Paris, 1846. 324 p.

        BN DLC MH   1859: BM NN   1860: NcD

1052   Speers, Laura B. *See* Morris, Mrs. Martha (Marlowe).

1053   Spence, J. C.
        The Dawn of Civilization; or, England in the Nineteenth Century. London, 1897. 176 p.

        BM

1054 ——————.

L'Aurore de la Civilisation, ou, l'Angleterre au XXe Siècle. Traduit de l'Anglais par A. Nauquet & G. Mossé. Paris, 1900. 279 p.

BM BN CtY ICU NcD

1055 Spence, Thomas, 1750–1814.

A Supplement to the History of Robinson Crusoe, Being the History of Crusonia . . . down to the Present Time . . . With an History of the Rise and Progress of Learning in Lilliput, the History of the Mercolians, and an Account of What Passed on a Journey with Old Zigzag. The Whole by T. Spence. Newcastle, Eng., 1782. 24 p.

BM

1056 ——————.

"Dhĕ K'onst'itush'un 'ov Sp'ensone 'a, a kŭntre ĭn Fare Lănd, sĭtuatĕd bĕtwen Utope'a and Oshean'a: brŏŏt frŏm dhĕns bi K'apt. Sw'alo. 'And prĭntĕd ĭn dhĕ Spĕnsoneăn mănr." 27 p. In Pig's Meat; or, Lessons for the Swinish Multitude, vol. 3. London, 1793.

BM CSmH CtY ICN MH

1057 ——————.

The Constitution of a Perfect Commonwealth: Being the French Constitution of 1793, Amended, and Rendered Entirely Conformable to the Whole Rights of Man. London, 1798. 24 p.

BM

1058 ——————.

The Constitution of Spensonia: a Country in Fairyland Situated Between Utopia and Oceana, Brought from Thence by Captain Swallow. London, 1803.

CSmH

1059 ——————.

"The Constitution of Spensonia. . . ." In Trial of Thomas Spence . . . with his Description of Spensonia, Constitution of

Spensonia, edited by Arthur W. Waters. Leamington Spa, Eng., 1917. 131 p.

BM DLC ICN MH NN

1060   Spronck, Maurice, 1864–.
        L'An 330 de la République; XXIIe Siècle de l'Ère Chrétienne.
        Paris, 1894. 140 p.

        BM BN MH

1061   [Stanislaus I, Lesczinski, king of Poland], 1677–1766.
        Entretien d'un Européan avec un Insulaire du Royaume de
        Dumocala. Paris (?), 1752. 158 p.

        BM   1754: BN

1062   [————].
        "Entretien d'un Européan. . . ." In *Oeuvres du Philosophe*
        Bienfaisant, 3:223–88. Paris, 1763.

        BM ICN NcD

1063   Stanley, William Ford Robinson, 1829–1909.
        The Case of The[odore] *Fox: Being His Prophecies under*
        Hypnotism of the Period Ending A.D. 1950. A Political Utopia.
        London, 1903. 199 p.

        BM ICN NcD NN

1064   Stapledon, William Olaf, 1886–.
        Last and First Men. A Story of the Near and Far Future. Lon-
        don, 1930. 355 p.

        BM DLC ICN ICU NcD   1931: CtY MH NN

1065   ————.
        Last Men in London. London, 1932. 312 p.

        BM ICN NcD

1066   Stauffer, Mack.
        Humanity and the Mysterious Knight. Boston, 1914. 295 p.

        DLC ICN NcD

1067 Stevens, Isaac Newton, 1858–.
The Liberators; a Story of Future American Politics. New York, 1908. 352 p.

CSmH CtY DLC ICN ICU MH NcD NN

1068 Stevenson, Dorothy Emily.
The Empty World. A Romance of the Future. London, 1936. 312 p. (Published in the U.S. as *The World in Spell.* New York, 1936. 298 p.)

BM NcD

1069 Stiblin, Gaspar (Gasparus Stiblinus), 1526–1597.
. . . de Eudaemonensium Republica Commentariolus. Basle, 1555. 127 p.

BN

1070 ———.
. . . de Eudamonensium Republica Commentariolus. Edited by Luigi Firpo. Turin, 1959. 122 p.

Bod ICN ICU NcD

1071 Stone, Mrs. C. H.
One of "Berrian's" Novels. New York, 1890. 210 p.

DLC MH NN

1072 Straus, Ralph, 1882–.
The Dust Which Is God: an Undimensional Adventure. Norwich, Eng., 1907. 62 p.

BM CtY NN

1073 ———.
5000 A.D. A Review and an Excursion . . . Read Before ye Sette of Odd Volumes at Oddenino's Imperial Restaurant on Jan. 24th, 1911. London, 1911. 56 p.

BM CtY DLC ICN MH NN

1074 Ströbel, Heinrich.
Die Erste Milliarde der Zweiten Billion. Die Gesellschaft der Zukunft. Berlin, 1919. 350 p.

BM DLC NN

1075 Strongi'th'arm, Charles (*pseud.*). *See* Armstrong, Charles Wicksteed.

1076 [Stubbes, George], *fl.* 1697–1737.
A New Adventure of Telemachus. London, 1731. 56 p.

BM CtY DLC ICN MH NcD

1077 Sullivan, Philip Aloysius, 1882–.
Man Finds the Way. New York, 1939. 217 p.

DLC NN NcD

1078 Sumner, Park.
Tomorrow Comes; a Story of Hope. Akron, Ohio, 1934. 44 p.

DLC NN

1079 Sutherland, James Runcieman, 1900–.
The Narrative of Jasper Weeple, Being an Account of His Strange Journey to the Land of Midanglia. London, 1930. 260 p.

BM MH NcD

1080 Sweven, Godfrey (*pseud.*). *See* Brown, John Macmillan.

1081 [Swift, Jonathan], 1667–1745.
Travels into Several Remote Nations of the World, in Four Parts, by Lemuel Gulliver. 2 vols. London, 1726.

BM CSmH CtY DLC ICN ICU MH NcD NN
1735: BN (Works)

1082 Swift, Morrison Isaac, 1856–.
The Horroboos. Boston, 1911. 241 p.

BN DLC MH NcD NN

1083 Symmes, John Cleves. *See* Seaborn, Capt. Adam.

1084 Tangent, Patrick Quinn (*pseud.*). *See* Phelps, George Hamilton.

1085   Tarbouriech, Ernest.
La Cité Future; Essai d'une Utopie Scientifique. Paris, 1902. 484 p.
BN CtY DLC ICN MH   1910: ICU NcD NN

1086   Tarde, Jean Gabriel de, 1843–1904.
Fragment d'Histoire Future. Paris, 1896. 52 p. Paris, 1904. 138 p.
BN   1904: BM MH NcD   1905: CtY

1087   ————.
Underground Man. Translated by Cloudesley Brereton. London, 1905. 198 p.
BM DLC NcD

1088   Tayler, John Lionel, 1874–1930.
The Last of My Race. A Dream of the Future. Lincoln, Eng., 1924. 131 p.
BM NN

1089   Taylor, William Alexander, 1837–1912.
Intermere. Columbus, Ohio, 1901. 148 p.
DLC ICN NcD   1902: NN

1090   Teed, Cyrus Romulus Reed (*pseud.* Lord Chester), 1838–1908.
The Great Red Dragon; or, the Flaming Devil of the Orient. Estero, Fla., 1909. 148 p.
DLC NN   1916: BM

1091   Teluccini, Mario (*pseud.* Il Bernia).
Artemidoro. Dove si Contengono le Grandezze de Gli Antipodi. Venice, 1566. 467 p.
BM CSmH MH

1092   [Terrasson, Jean, abbé], 1670–1750.
Sethos, Histoire ou Vie Tirée des Monumens Anecdotes de l'Ancienne Égypte; Traduite d'un Manuscrit Grec. 3 vols. Paris, 1731.
BM BN CSmH NcD NN   1732: CtY ICN   1767: MH

1093   [————].
The Life of Sethos. Translated by Thomas Lediard. 2 vols. London, 1732.
BM DLC ICN ICU MH NN

1094   Thirion, Émile Ambroise, 1825–.
Neustria, Utopie Individualiste. Paris, 1901. 375 p.
BN NN

1095   Thiusen, Ismar (*pseud.*). *See* Macnie, John.

1096   Thomas, Chauncey, 1822–1898.
The Crystal Button, or, Adventures of Paul Prognosis in the Forty-Ninth Century. Boston and New York, 1891. 302 p.
BM CSmH CtY DLC ICN ICU MH NcD NN

1097   [Thomson, William], 1746–1817.
The Man in the Moon, or Travels into the Lunar Regions, by the Man of the People. 2 vols. London, 1783.
BM BN CtY DLC ICN MH NcD

1098   [————].
Mammuth; or, Human Nature Displayed on a Grand Scale: in a Tour with the Tinkers into the Inland Parts of Africa. By the Man in the Moon. 2 vols. London, 1789.
Bod CtY MH

1099   Tillyard, Aelfrida Catharine Wetenhall.
Concrete. A Story of Two Hundred Years Hence. London, 1930 . 288 p.
BM MH

1100   Tincker, Mary Agnes, 1831–1907.
San Salvador. Boston and New York, 1892. 335 p.
BM CSmH DLC ICN MH NcD NN

1101   Tiphaigne de la Roche, Charles François, 1729–1774.
Giphantie. Babylone (i.e., Paris), 1760. 176 + 174 p.
BM BN DLC MH   1761: NcD

1102   ————.

Giphantia; or a View of What Has Passed, What Is Now Passing, and, During the Present Century, What Will Pass in the World. London, 1760–61. 126 p.

BM CSmH CtY DLC ICN MH NN

1103   ————.

L'Empire des Zaziris sur les Humains, ou la Zazirocratie. Pékin (i.e., Paris), 1761. 121 p.

BM BN DLC ICN

1104   ————.

Histoire des Galligènes. 2 vols. in 1. Amsterdam, 1765.

BM BN   1770: ICN NcD

1105   Tracy, Louis, 1863–1928.
An American Emperor; the Story of the Fourth Empire of France. New York, 1897. 424 p.

BM CSmH DLC MH NcD   n.d. (French): BN

1106   ————.

The Lost Provinces; How Vansittart Came Back to France. New York, 1898. 408 p.

BM CSmH DLC NcD NN

1107   "The Travels and Adventures of a Philosopher in the Famous Empire of Hulee. From an old Ms., A.D. 2070." *Fraser's Magazine* 3 (1871):703–17 (new series).

BM BN CtY DLC ICN ICU MH NcD NN

1108   Trevena, John (*pseud.*) . *See* Henham, Ernest George.

1109   Trevor, Philip Christian William.
A Prince of the People: a Romance of Modern Royalty. London, 1904. 299 p.

BM

1110   Trollope, Anthony, 1815–1882.
        The Fixed Period. 2 vols. Edinburgh and London, 1882. [First
        published in *Blackwoods Magazine,* October 1881-March 1882.]
        BM CSmH CtY DLC ICN ICU MH NcD NN

1111   Trygaeus (*pseud.*).
        The United States of the World. London, 1916. 63 p.
        BM ICU NN

1112   [Tucker, George] (*pseud.* Joseph Atterley), 1775–1861.
        *A Voyage to the Moon: with Some Account of the Manners
        and Customs, Science and Philosophy, of the People of Moro-
        sofia, and Other Lunarians.* New York, 1827. 264 p.
        CSmH CtY DLC ICN MH NcD

1113   [————].
        "A Century Hence: or a Romance of 1941." An unpublished
        manuscript in the University of Virginia Library. [*See* Jay B.
        Hubbell, *The South in American Literature* (Durham, N.C.,
        1954), pp. 252–54.]

1114   Tuckwell, William, 1829–1919.
        The New Utopia, or England in 1985. Birmingham, 1885. 16 p.
        BM

1115   Twain, Mark (*pseud.*). *See* Clemens, Samuel Langhorne.

1116   Tweed, Thomas Frederic, 1890–.
        Blind Mouths. London, 1934. 386 p.
        BM DLC

1117   [Tyssot de Patot, Simon] (*pseud.* Jaques Massé), 1655–1728(?).
        Voyages et Avantures de Jaques Massé. Bordeaux (The
        Hague?), 1710. 508 p.
        BM BN CtY DLC ICN MH NcD NN   1760: CSmH

1118   [————].
        The Travels and Adventures of James Massey. . . . Translated
        by Stephen Whatley. London, 1733. 318 p.
        BM BN CtY ICN ICU NcD

1119   [————].
         The Travels and Adventures of James Massey. . . . Translated
         by Monsieur Bayle. London, 1743. 370 p.

         BM DLC ICN ICU NN

1120   [————].
         *La Vie, les Avantures, et le Voyage de Groenland du Révérend
         Père Cordelier Pierre de Mesange. Avec une Relation Bien
         Circonstanciée de l'Origine, de l'Histoire, des Moeurs, et du
         Paradis des Habitans de Pole Artique.* 2 vols. Amsterdam, 1720.

         BM CtY DLC ICN MH NN

1121   Unitas (*pseud.*).
         The Dream City. London, 1920. 121 p.

         BM MH

1122   *Utopia: or, Apollo's Golden Days*. Dublin, 1747. 14 p.
         CSmH

1123   [Vairasse, Denis (Veiras, d'Alais, Allais, Veirasse d'Alais)] (*pseud.*
         Captain Siden), 1630(?)–1700(?).
         *The History of the Sevarites or Sevarambi: a Nation Inhabiting
         Part of the Third Continent, Commonly Called, Terrae Aus-
         trales Incognitae.* Translated by A. Roberts. London, 1675.
         140 p. (Probably written in English by Vairasse.)

         Bod CSmH CtY DLC MH NcD NN

1124   [————].
         L'Histoire des Sevarambres. 2 vols. in 1. Paris, 1677.

         BN MH   1680: BM   1702: CtY   1715: NcD
         1716: DLC ICN ICU NN   1787: CSmH

1125   Vander Neck, J. (*pseud.*). *See* Burgh, James.

1126   van Dovski, Lee (*pseud.*). *See* Lewandowski, Herbert.

1127   van Sloetten. *See* Sloetten.

1128   [Varennes de Mondasse, de.]
        La Découverte de l'Empire de Cantahar. Paris, 1730. 373 p.
        BN CtY DLC ICN NN

1129   [Vargas Vila, José María], 1860–1933.
        Los Estetos de Teopolis. Madrid, 1918. 232 p.
        Biblioteca Nacional, Madrid   1922: DLC
        Works: CtY NcD

1130   Vassos, John, 1898–, and Ruth Vassos.
        Ultimo; an Imaginative Narration of Life Under the Earth.
        New York, 1930. 52 p.
        CtY DLC NcD NN

1131   Vaughan, Herbert Millingchamp, 1870–1948.
        Meleager: a Fantasy. London, 1916. 323 p.
        BM NcD NN

1132   [Vaulet, Clément] (*pseud.* Clément Vautel), 1876–.
        Voyage au Pays des Snobs. Paris, 1928. 296 p.
        BN NN

1133   Veiras. *See* Vairasse, Denis.

1134   Verdaguer, Mario, 1893–.
        La Isla de Oro, Novela. Barcelona, 1926. 300 p.
        DLC NcD   1954 (French): BN

1135   Verne, Jules, 1828–1905.
        *Les Cinq Cents Millions de la Bégum, Suivi de les Révoltés de
        la "Bounty."* Paris, 1879. 185 p.
        BM BN DLC   188–: MH NN

1136   ————.
        The 500 Millions of the Begum. New York, 1879. 23 p. *The
        Begum's Fortune.* London, 1880.
        DLC   1911: ICU   1958: NN   1960: NcD

1137 ———.
"La Journée d'un Journaliste Américain en 2889." In *Hier et Demain. Contes et Nouvelles.* Paris, 1910. 316 p.

BN DLC

1138 Versou, Jozef.
Nieuwe Reis Naar Utopia; Fantastisch Verhaal. Brussels, 1944. 119 p.

DLC NN

1139 Vetsch, Jakob (*pseud.* Jakob Mundus).
Die Sonnenstadt; ein Roman aus der Zukunft, von Mundus. Zurich, 1922. 406 p.

DLC   1923: BM NcD NN

1140 [Vickers, John] (*pseud.* Jaido Morata).
The New Koran of the Pacifican Friendhood. London, 1861. 573 p.

BM CtY DLC NN

1141 [Villeneuve, de] (*pseud.* Listonai).
Le Voyageur Philosophe dans un Pais Inconnu aux Habitants de la Terre. Multa Incredibilia Vers. Multa Credibilia Falsa. Par Mr. de Listonai. 2 vols. Amsterdam, 1761.

CtY ICN MH NcD   1771: BN

1142 Vinton, Arthur Dudley, 1852–1906.
Looking Further Backward. Being a Series of Lectures Delivered to the Freshman Class at Shawmut College, by Professor Won Lung Li (Successor of Prof. Julian West). Albany, N.Y., 1890. 236 p.

BM CtY DLC ICN MH NcD NN

1143 Vogel, Sir Julius, 1835–1899.
Anno Domini 2000; or, Woman's Destiny. London, 1889. 331 p.

BM NcD

1144   Volney, Constantin François Chasseboeuf, comte de, 1757–1820.
Les Ruines, ou Méditation sur les Révolutions des Empires.
Paris, 1791. 410 p.

    BM   1792: CtY DLC ICN MH NN   1826: ICU NcD

1145   ————.
The Ruins: or, a Survey of the Revolution of Empires. London,
1795. 394 p.

    BM NcD   1796: DLC MH   1799: CSmH CtY
    1802: NN   1807: ICN   18–: ICU

1146   Voltaire, François Marie Arouet de, 1694–1778.
Le Micromégas de Mr. de Voltaire. London, 1752. 257 p.
(Probably written in 1739.)

    BM CtY   1753: MH   n.d.: BN

1147   ————.
Micromegas, a Comic Romance. London, 1753. 252 p.

    BM CSmH CtY DLC ICN ICU MH

1148   ————.
Voltaire's Micromegas. Edited by Ira O. Wade. Princeton, N.J.,
1950. 190 p.

    BM CtY DLC ICN ICU MH NcD

1149   von Himmel, Ernest (*pseud.*). *See* Petersilea, Carlyle.

1150   Vonnegut, Kurt, 1922–.
Player Piano. New York, 1952. 295 p.

    CtY DLC ICU NcD NN   1953: BM Bod MH

1151   von Swartwout, William Henry.
*Declaration of Principles and Proclamations of Emancipation
by the President of the New Columbia United State (of the
World).* London and New York, 1887. 131 p. [Later editions
are titled *New Columbia* and *Olombia*.]

    BM DLC   1893: NN

1152   [Vose, Reuben] (*pseud.* Invisible Sam).
       Despotism; or, the Last Days of the American Republic. New
       York, 1856. 463 p.
       CSmH CtY DLC ICN ICU NcD NN

1153   *A Voyage to the Moon. Strongly Recommended to All Lovers of
       Real Freedom.* London, 1793. 39 p.
       DLC

1154   *A Voyage to the New Island Fonseca, near Barbadoes. With Some
       Observations Made in a Cruize Among the Leward Islands.
       In Letters from Two Captains of Turkish Men of War, Driven
       Thither in the Year 1707. Translated out of Turkish and
       French.* London, 1708. 44 p.
       DLC ICN

1155   *A Voyage to the World in the Centre of the Earth Giving an Ac-
       count of the Manners, Customs, Laws, Government and Re-
       ligion of the Inhabitants.* London, 1755. 275 p.
       BM DLC

1156   W., E.
       *The Island of Anarchy; A Fragment of History in the 20th
       Century.* Reading, Eng., 1887. 105 p.
       MH NcD

1157   W., R. *See* Walker, Richard.

1158   Wahrenburg, Constantinus von. *See* Sinold, Philipp Balthasar.

1159   Walker, John Brisben (*pseud.* Sir Robert Harton), 1847–1931.
       "A Brief History of Altruria." *The Cosmopolitan,* vol. 20, No-
       vember 1895-March 1896.
       BM BN CtY DLC ICN ICU MH NcD NN

1160   [Walker, Richard], 1791–1870.
       Oxford in 1888: a Fragmentary Dream, by a Sub-Utopian.

Published from the Original MS. by the Editor, R. W. Oxford, 1838. 70 p.

BM Bod CtY

1161　Wall, John W. (*pseud.* Sarban).
The Sound of His Horn. London, 1952. 153 p.

BM

1162　Walter, Henry (*pseud.*). *See* Röcken, Kurt Walter.

1163　[Ward, Edward], 1667–1731 (attributed author).
A New Voyage to the Island of Fools. Representing the Policy, Government, and Present State of the Stultitians. London, 1713. 62 p.

Bod CSmH ICN MH

1164　[Warde, Beatrice Lamberton (Becker)] (*pseud.* Paul Beaujon), 1900–.
Peace Under Earth: Dialogues from the Year 1946. London, 1938. 46 p. (Privately printed in 1937 as *The Shelter of Bedlam.*)

Bod NN　　1937: DLC

1165　Warner, Rex, 1905–.
The Wild Goose Chase. London, 1937. 442 p.

BM CtY DLC MH NcD NN　　1947: BN

1166　[Wasserburg, Philipp] (*pseud.* Philipp Laicus), 1827–1897.
Etwas Später! Forsetzung von Bellamy's Rückblick aus dem Jahre 2000. Mainz, 1891. 208 p.

BM MH

1167　Watlock, W. A.
The Next Ninety-three, or Crown, Commune and Colony Told in a Citizen's Diary. London, 1886. 36 p.

BM

1168　Watts, Newman, 1895–.
The Man Who Could Not Sin. London, 1938. 223 p.
DLC ICN NcD NN　　1939: BM

1169   Waugh, Evelyn, 1903–.
Love Among the Ruins. A Romance of the Near Future. London, 1953. 51 p.
BM BN CSmH CtY DLC ICU MH NcD NN

1170   Webb, Jane (Loudon). *See* Loudon, Mrs. Jane (Webb).

1171   Webster, R. M.
One Wise Rich Man. A Parable. N.p., 18–. 12 p.
ICU

1172   Wehr, Werner (*pseud.*). *See* Gartmann, Heinz.

1173   Weitling, Wilhelm Christian, 1808–1871.
Die Menschheit, Wie Sie Ist und Wie Sein Sollte. Bern, 1845. 54 p.
DLC NcD   1854: NN   1895: ICU

1174   Welcome, S. Byron.
From Earth's Centre; a Polar Gateway Message. Chicago, 1894. 274 p.
DLC MH   1895: CtY ICU NN

1175   Wells, Herbert George, 1866–1946.
[H. G. Wells presents a special problem since all his numerous works have utopian significance; those listed seem most important for this bibliography.]
The Time Machine, an Invention. London, 1895. 152 p.
BM CSmH CtY DLC ICN MH NcD NN   1911: BN

1176   ————.
When the Sleeper Wakes. London, 1899. 328 p.
BM CSmH CtY DLC ICN ICU MH NcD NN
1906: BN

1177   ————.
The First Men in the Moon. London, 1901. 342 p.
BM CSmH CtY DLC ICN MH NcD NN   1902: BN

1178 —————.
A Modern Utopia. London, 1905. 393 p.

BM CSmH CtY DLC ICN MH NcD NN   1909: ICU
1912: BN

1179 —————.
The War in the Air. London, 1908. 389 p.

BM CSmH CtY DLC ICN ICU MH NcD NN
1911: BN

1180 —————.
The World Set Free: a Story of Mankind. London, 1914. 286 p.

BM CSmH CtY DLC ICN ICU MH NcD NN

1181 —————.
Men Like Gods. London, 1923. 304 p.

BM BN CSmH CtY DLC ICN ICU MH NcD NN

1182 —————.
The Open Conspiracy; Blueprints for a World Revolution.
London, 1928. 156 p.

BM BN CSmH CtY DLC ICN ICU MH NcD NN

1183 Werner, Isidore. See Douglass, Ellsworth.

1184 Whately, Richard. See Fox, Lady Mary.

1185 Whatley, Stephen. See de Ramsay, Andrew Michael.

1186 Whiteing, Richard, 1840–1928.
The Island; or, an Adventure of a Person of Quality. London,
1888. 290 p.

BM CtY ICN MH NcD   1899: DLC ICU NN

1187 [Whiting, Sydney.]
Heliondé; or, Adventures in the Sun. London, 1855. 424 p.

BM   1866: MH

1188   Whitmore, H. (*pseud.* Lemuel Gulliver, jun.).
        Modern Gulliver's Travels. Lilliput: Being a New Journey to That Celebrated Island . . . From the Year 1702 (When They Were First Discovered and Visited by Captain Lemuel Gulliver, the Father of the Compiler of This Work) to the Present Aera 1796. London, 1796. 226 p.

        BM CtY DLC ICN ICU NN

1189   Wieland, Christoph Martin, 1733–1813.
        Der Goldne Spiegel, oder die Könige von Scheschian, eine Wahre Geschichte. Aus dem Scheschianischen Übersetzt. 2 vols. Leipzig, 1772.

        BM CtY   1777: DLC   Works: BN ICN ICU MH NcD NN

1190   ————.
        Die Abderiten, eine Sehr Wahrscheinliche Geschichte. 2 vols. Weimar, 1776.

        ICU   1781: BM   1782: DLC   1796: MH
        Works: BN CtY ICN NcD NN

1191   ————.
        The Republic of Fools: Being the History of the State and People of Abdera in Thrace. Translated by H. Christmas. 2 vols. London, 1861.

        BM CtY DLC NN

1192   Wilbrandt, Conrad.
        Des Herrn Friedrich Ost Erlebnisse in der Welt Bellamy's. Mitteilungen aus den Jahren 2001 und 2002. Weimar, 1891. 212 p.

        BM DLC MH NN

1193   ————.
        Mr. East's Experiences in Mr. Bellamy's World; Records of the Years 2001 and 2002. Translated by Mary J. Safford. New York, 1891. 255 p.

        BM CSmH DLC ICN NcD NN

1194   Wilkie, J.
        The Vision of Nehemiah Sintram. London, 1902. 96 p.
        BM

1195   Willebrord (*pseud.*).
        Ein Blik in de Toekomst. Middelburg, Netherlands, 1871. 52 p.
        BM NN

1196   [Williams, David Rhys] (*pseud.* Gan "Index").
        Y dyn oddimewn; neu, am dro i fyd y tumewn-ogiaid. Utica,
        N.Y., 1913. 163 p.
        DLC

1197   Williams, Frederic Condé.
        "Utopia. The Story of a Strange Experience." In *The Cam-
        bridge Christmas Annual,* vol. 1 (1895), 72 p.
        BM

1198   Williams, Morris (*pseud.*). *See* Gildon, Charles and Killigrew,
        Thomas.

1199   Willoughby, Frank, 1866–.
        *Through the Needle's Eye; a Narrative of the Restoration of
        the Davidic Kingdom of Israel in Palestine with Jesus Christ
        as King.* New York, 1925. 155 p.
        DLC NcD

1200   Wilson, Hardy.
        Kurrajong, Sit-Look-See. Kew, Australia, 1954. 48 p.
        NN

1201   Wilson, John Anthony Burgess (*pseud.* Anthony Burgess).
        The Wanting Seed. London, 1962. 285 p.
        BM BN CtY ICU MH NcD NN   1963: DLC

1202   Wilson, Philip Whitwell, 1875–.
        Newtopia. The World We Want. New York, 1941. 219 p.
        BM CtY DLC ICN ICU MH NcD NN

1203   Winch, Edgar.
       The Mountain of Gold. London, 1928. 287 p.
       BM DLC

1204   Windsor, William.
       Loma, a Citizen of Venus. St. Paul, 1897. 429 p.
       BM NcD

1205   [Wise, C.]
       Darkness and Dawn. The Peaceful Birth of a New Age. London, 1884. 141 p.
       BM

1206   *Der Wohleingerichtete Staat. Des Bishero von Vielen Gesuchten aber Nicht Gefundenen Königreichs Ophir.* Leipzig, 1699. 608 p. (Some copies, of the same date, have different title pages.)
       BM ICN

1207   Wolf, Howard, 1902–.
       Greener Pastures; a Fable of Past, Present and Future. Caldwell, Idaho, 1936. 107 p.
       CtY DLC ICN MH NcD NN

1208   Wolfe, Bernard, 1915–.
       Limbo '90. London, 1952. 438 p.
       CtY DLC ICN ICU NcD NN   1953: BM Bod
       1955 (French): BN

1209   *A Woman's Utopia. By a Daughter of Eve.* London, 1931. 92 p.
       BM NN

1210   Wonder, William (*pseud.*). *See* Kirwan, Thomas.

1211   Wood, George.
       Future Life; or, Scenes in Another World. Boston, 1858. 359 p. (1849 edition titled *The Gates Wide Open.*)
       CtY DLC ICU MH NN   1869: BM CSmH ICN NcD

1212   Wooldridge, Charles William, 1847–.
        Perfecting the Earth; a Piece of Possible History. Cleveland,
        1902. 326 p.

        DLC ICN ICU MH NcD NN

1213   "Worlds to Watch and Ward." (*Anon.*). In *The Quest for Utopia,*
        by Glenn Negley and J. Max Patrick, chap. 33. New York,
        1952, 1962, 1971.

        Bod CSmH CtY DLC ICN ICU MH NcD NN

1214   [Worley, Frederick U.] (*pseud.* Benefice).
        *Three Thousand Dollars a Year. Moving Forward, or How
        We Got There . . . from the Advance Sheets of a History
        . . . to Be Published in the Year 2001.* Washington, D.C., 1890.
        104 p.

        DLC ICN

1215   Wright, Austin Tappen, 1883–1931.
        Islandia. New York, 1942. 1013 p. (*See* Davenport, Basil.)

        CtY DLC ICN MH NcD NN   1958: ICU

1216   Wright, Frances (Mme. Frances [Wright] D'Arusmont), 1795–1852.
        *A Few Days in Athens, Being the Translation of a Greek Manu-
        script Discovered in Herculaneum.* New York, 1822. 166 p.

        BM Bod CtY DLC ICU   1831: MH NN   1853: NcD

1217   Wright, Sydney Fowler (*pseud.* Sydney Fowler), 1874–.
        The World Below. London, 1929. 314 p.

        BM Bod DLC NcD   1930: CtY MH NN   1949: ICN
        1953 (French): BN

1218   ———.
        The Adventure of Wyndham Smith. London, 1938. 284 p.

        BM Bod NcD

1219   Wurmsaam, Vermelio (*pseud.*). *See* Callenbach, Franz.

1220 [Wybraniec, Peter Frank] (*pseud.* Dr. Raphael W. Leonhart), 1882-.
Speratia, the Land of Hope. Boston, 1935. 271 p.
DLC MH NcD NN   1941: ICU

1221 Wyndham, John (*pseud.*). *See* Harris, John Beynon.

1222 X (*pseud.*). *See* Fawkes, Frank Attfield.

1223 Younghusband, Sir Francis Edward, 1863-.
The Coming Country. A Pre-Vision. London, 1928. 309 p.
Bod ICN NcD NN   1929: CtY DLC

1224 [Zacharie de Lisieux] (Louis Fontaines, Pietro Firmiano, Petrus Firmianus), 1582-1661.
Relation du Pays de Jansenie, ou Il Est Traitte des Singularitez Qui S'y Trouvent, des Coustumes, Moeurs et Religion des Habitans. Paris, 1660. 118 p.
BM NN   1681: DLC

1225 [————].
A Relation of the Country of Jansenia, Wherein Is Treated of the Singularities Founded Therein. London, 1668.
BM CtY ICN

1226 Zamiatin, Evgenii Ivanovich, 1884-1937.
We. Translated by Gregory Zilboorg. New York, 1924. 286 p.
DLC ICN ICU MH NcD NN   1952: CtY
1929((French): BN

1227 Zelis, the Persian (*pseud.*).
Celenia: or, the History of Hyempsal, King of Numidia. 2 vols. London, 1736.
BM ICN ICU MH   1740: CSmH

149

1228   Zola, Émile Édouard Charles Antoine, 1840–1902.
Travail. Paris, 1901. 666 p.

BN CtY DLC ICN ICU MH NcD NN

1229   ————.
Travail. Labor, a Novel. New York and London, 1901. 604 p.

Bod CtY DLC MH NN

1230   Zuccolo, Lodovico, 1568–1630.
Considerationi Politiche e Morali sopra Cento Oracoli l'Illustri Personaggi Antichi. Venice, 1621. 404 p.

BM   1623: NcD

1231   ————.
Dialoghi . . . ne'Quali con Varieta di Eruditione si Scoprono Nuovi, e Vaghi Pensieri Filosofici Morali, e Politici. Perugia, 1625.

ICN ICU

1232   ————.
La Republica d'Evandria e Altri Dialoghi Politici. Edited by Rodolfo de Mattei. Rome, 1944. (Reprint of *Consideratoni . . .* and *Dialoghi. . . .*)

DLC

Works Influential
in Utopian Thought

1233   Ablancourt. *See* Perrot d'Ablancourt, Nicholas.

1234   Adam, Paul Auguste Marie, 1862–1920.
The Future City, Artistic and Scientific World Centre. Paris, 1914. 24 p.
DLC

1235   Albergati, Fabio, 1538–1606.
Dei Discorsi Politici di F. Albergati Libri Cinque. Nei Quali Viene Riprovata la Dottrina Politica di Gio. Bodino, e Difesa Quella d'Aristotele. Rome, 1602. 427 p.
BM BN ICN   1603: ICU   1664: NcD

1236   ————.
La Republica Regia del Sig. Fabio Albergati al Serenissimo Prencipe D. Francesco Maria II Duca d'Urbino VI. Bologna, 1627. 342 p.
BM BN CSmH ICN NcD

1237   *Annus Sophiae Jubilaeus, the Sophick Constitution: or, the Evil Customs of the World Reform'd. A Dialogue, Between a Philadelft and a Citizen.* London, 1700.
CtY

1238   Aspinwall, William, *fl.* 1630–1662.
A Brief Description of the Fifth Monarchy, or Kingdome that Shortly Is to Come into the World. London, 1653. 14 p.
BM NN   1794: DLC

1239   [Aubignac, François Hédelin, abbé d'], 1604–1676.
Histoire du Temps, ou Relation du Royaume de Coqueterie, Extraite du Dernier Voyage des Holandois aux Indes du Levant. Paris, 1654. 84 p.
BM BN   1655: CtY DLC   1788: CSmH   1789: ICN

1240   [————].
Lettre d'Ariste à Cléonte, Contenant l'Apologie de l'"Histoire du Temps," ou, la Défense du "Royaume de Coqueterie." Paris, 1659. 120 p.
BN   1660: BM CtY

1241   [————].
> *Macarise; ou, la Reyne des Îsles Fortunées. Histoire Allégorique Contenant la Philosophie Morale des Stoïques Sous le Voile de Plusieurs Aventures Agréables en Forme de Roman.* 2 vols. Paris, 1664.
>
> BM BN MH

1242   [Bage, Robert], 1728–1801.
> *Hermsprong; or, Man As He Is Not.* 2 vols. Dublin, 1796.
>
> BM CSmH CtY ICN   1799: MH   1803: DLC
> 1820: ICU

1243   [————].
> *Hermsprong.* . . . Edited by Vaughan Wilkins. London and New York, 1951. 248 p.
>
> BM CtY DLC ICU MH NcD NN

1244   [————].
> *Hermsprong.* . . . Edited by Vaughan Wilkins. London, 1960. 262 p.
>
> BM CtY DLC MH NcD NN

1245   Balsdon, John Percy Vyvian Dacre, 1901–.
> *Sell England?* London, 1936. 278 p.
>
> BM NcD NN

1246   [Bandelloni, Cesare Emilio] (*pseud.* Ciofro).
> *La Umana Società in un Sistema Corporative Autonomo Che Offre Sempre a Tutti Lavoro, Giutizia e Pace. Nuova Edizione dell'Opera "La Profezia Finale."* Florence, 1938. 377 p.
>
> DLC ICU

1247   Bangs, John Kendrick, 1862–1922.
> *Alice in Blunderland: an Iridescent Dream.* New York, 1907. 124 p.
>
> BM CSmH CtY DLC ICU MH NcD NN

1248   [Banim, John], 1798–1842.
Revelations of the Dead-Alive. London, 1824. 376 p.
BM DLC

1249   Barclay, John (Johannes Barclaiius), 1582–1621.
Euphormionis Lusinini J. Barclaii Satyricon. Paris, 1605. 126 ff.
BN   1623: BM CtY ICN   1628: CSmH NcD
1634: ICU NN   1637: MH

1250   ————.
Euphormio's Satyricon. Translated by Paul Turner. London, 1954. 158 p.
BM CtY DLC ICN ICU MH NcD NN

1251   ————.
Ioannis Barclaii Argenis. Paris, 1621. 1208 p. (Numerous editions and translations.)
BM BN CSmH CtY MH   1622: ICN   1627: DLC
1630: ICU NcD   1659: NN

1252   ————.
Barclay His Argenis: or, the Loves of Poliarchus and Argenis. Translated by Kingsmill Long. London, 1625. 404 p.
BM CtY ICN ICU MH   1636: BN

1253   ————.
Argenis . . . the Prose by Sir Robert Le Grys and the Verses by Thomas May. London, 1628. 489 p.
BM Bod CtY MH NcD

1254   [Bassett, Edward Barnard] (*pseud.* Beta).
The Model Town; or, the Right and Progressive Organization of Industry for the Production of Material and Moral Wealth. Cambridge, 1869. 104 p.
DLC ICU MH NcD NN

1255   Baxter, Garrett.
Rosma. Norfolk, Va., 1932. 100 p.
DLC

1256   Baxter, Richard, 1615–1691.
        A Holy Commonwealth; or Political Aphorisms, Opening the
        True Principles of Government: for the Healing of the Mis-
        takes, and Resolving the Doubts, that Most Endanger and
        Touble England at This Time: (If Yet There May Be Hope).
        Written by Richard Baxter at the Invitation of James Harring-
        ton, Esquire. London, 1659. 517 p.

        BM BN CSmH CtY DLC ICN ICU MH

1257   Beacon, Richard, *fl.* 1594.
        Solon His Follie, or a Politique Discourse Touching the Refor-
        mation of Common-Weales Conquered, Declined, or Corrupted.
        Oxford, 1594. 114 p.

        BM CSmH CtY ICN MH

1258   Becerra Ochoa, Gamaliel.
        La Republica del Trabajo; Tesis que para Obtener el Titulo de
        Licenciado en Derecho, Presenta a la h. Consideracion sus
        Jurados, el Pasante de Derecho. Mexico City, 1932. (Typewrit-
        ten carbon copy.)

        DLC

1259   Beer, Samuel Hutchinson, 1911–.
        The City of Reason. Cambridge, Mass., 1949. 227 p.

        BM CtY DLC ICN ICU MH NcD NN

1260   Behrens, Joachimus.
        Exercitatio Politica de Optima Republica. Helmstadii, 1652.
        60 p.

        BM BN

1261   Bellamy, Charles Joseph, 1852–1910.
        An Experiment in Marriage. Albany, N.Y., 1889. 286 p.

        BM CtY DLC NcD NN

1262   Bellamy, Edward, 1850–1898.
        The Religion of Solidarity. Yellow Springs, Ohio, 1940. 43 p.
        (Written in 1874.)

        CSmH CtY DLC ICU MH NcD NN

1263   Bellarmino, Roberto Francesco Romolo, Saint (cardinal), 1542–1621.
De Officio Principis Christiani, Libri Tres. Rome, 1619. 492 p.

BM BN DLC ICN MH NcD

1264   [Bellers, John], 1654–1725.
Some Reasons for an European State, Proposed to the Powers of Europe, by an Universal Guarantee, and an Annual Congress, Senate, Dyet, or Parliament to Settle Any Disputes About the Bounds and Rights of Princes and States Hereafter. London, 1710. 21 p.

BM

1265   [————].
"Some Reasons . . . ." In *John Bellers, 1654–1725: Quaker, Economist and Social Reformer,* edited by A. Ruth Fry. London, 1935. 174 p.

BM CSmH CtY DLC ICN ICU MH NcD NN

1266   Bénard. *See* Bernard, Jean Frédéric.

1267   Bennett, Arthur.
The Dream of an Englishman. London, 1893. 190 p.

MH NN

1268   Beresford, John Davys, 1873–1947.
A Common Enemy. London, 1941. 208 p.

BM   1942: DLC NN

1269   ————.
"What Dreams May Come." London and Melbourne, 1941. 256 p.

BM DLC MH NN

1270   Berger-Bit, A.
L'Avenir, ou, le Nouveau Contrat Social. Paris, 1899. 140 p.

BN NN

1271   Bergeret, Stéphen.
        Plans de la Réalisation de la Société Future. Paris, 1912. 169 p.
        BN MH NN

1272   [Bernard, Jean Frédéric] (Bénard), *d.* 1752 (supposed author).
        Eloge de l'Enfer. Ouvrage Critique, Historique, et Moral. 2
        vols. The Hague, 1759.
        BM BN DLC ICN MH NcD   1777: CtY

1273   [————————].
        The Praise of Hell: or, a View of the Infernal Regions. Con-
        taining Some Account of the Advantages of That Place, with
        Respect to Its Antiquity, Situation, and Stability. . . . To Which
        is Added a Detail of the Laws, Government, and Constitution
        of Hell. 2 vols. London, 1760.
        BM CSmH CtY DLC ICU MH

1274   Beroalde de Verville, François, 1556–*ca.* 1612.
        L'Idée de la République. Paris, 1584. 102 p.
        BN CtY MH NN

1275   ————————.
        Le Moyen de Parvenir. Oeuvre Contenant la Raison de Tout
        Ce Qui A Ésté, Est et Sera, avec Démonstration Certaines et
        Necessaires Selon la Rencontre des Effets de Vertu. Paris, n.d.
        (*ca.* 1610). 617 p.
        BM   16–: ICN   1700: CSmH   1719: MH
        1732: BN CtY DLC   1739: ICU   1841: NcD NN

1276   ————————.
        Le Palais des Curieux. Auquel Sont Assemblés Plusieurs Di-
        versitez pour le Plaisir des Doctes, et le Bien de Ceux Qui
        Désirent Scavoir. Paris, 1612. 584 p.
        BM BN NcD

1277   Beroaldo, Filippo (Phillipus Beroaldus), 1453–1505.
        De Felicitate. Bologna, 1495. 36 leaves.
        BM BN CSmH MH   1499: CtY ICN ICU   1500: NcD
        1515: DLC

1278 —————.

Opusculum Eruditum Quo Continentur Declamatio Philosophi, Medici, Oratoris, de Excellentia Disceptatium, et Libellus de Optimo Statu et Principe. Bononiae (i.e., Bologna), 1497. 38 leaves.

BN Bod CtY ICN   1500: BM CSmH   1508: NcD
1509: ICU   1515: DLC

1279 Beta (pseud.). See Bassett, Edward Barnard.

1280 [Bethune, Philippe, comte de Selles et de Charost], 1561–1649.
Le Conseiller d'État; ou, Recueil des Plus Générales Considérations Servant au Maniment des Affaires Publiques. Paris, 1633. 503 p.

BM BN CtY ICN   1665: ICU

1281 [—————].
The Counsellor of Estate. . . . Translated by E. G. [Edward Grimstone]. London, 1634. 336 p.

BM CSmH CtY DLC ICN ICU MH NcD NN

1282 Bidermanus, Jacobus (Jakob Bidermann), ca. 1578–1639.
Utopia Didaci Bemardini. Dillingen, 1640. 396 p.

BM MH NN   1644: BN DLC   1668: ICN
1670: ICU

1283 Biese, Nicolas (Nicolaus Biesius), 1516–1572.
De Republica Libri Quatuor. Antwerp, 1556. 111 p.

BM BN MH   1564: DLC ICN

1284 [Bignon, Jean Paul, abbé] (pseud. William Hatchett, M. de Sandisson), 1662–1743.
Les Aventures d'Abdalla, Fils d'Hanif, Envoyé par le Sultan des Indes à le Découverte de l'Île de Borico . . . avec la Relation du Voyage de Rouschen, Dame Persane, dans l'Île Détournée. 2 vols. Paris, 1712–14.

BM BN   1723: ICN   1773: CtY MH   1785: NN

1285   [————].

The Adventures of Abdalla, Son of Hanif, Sent by the Sultan of the Indies, to Make a Discovery of the Island of Borico, Where the Fountain Which Restores Past Youth Is Supposed to Be Found. Also an Account of the Travels of Rouschen, a Persian Lady, to the Topsy-Turvy Island, Undiscovered to This Day . . . Done into English by William Hatchett, Gent. London, 1729. 169 p.

BM CSmH CtY DLC ICN MH NcD
1730: CSmH NN

1286   Boaistuau de Launay, Pierre (*pseud.* Chelidonius Tigurinus), *d.* 1566.
L'Histoire de Chelidonius Tigurinus sur l'Institution des Princes Chrestiens et Origine des Royaumes, Traduite de Latin en Français. Paris, 1556. 143 p.

MH   1559: BM BN CtY   1564: ICN

1287   ————.

A Most Excellent Hystorie of the Institution and Firste Beginning of Christian Princes . . . Englished by James Chillester. London, 1571. 199 p.

BM CSmH ICN

1288   Bodin, Jean, 1530–1596.
Les Six Livres de la République. Paris, 1576. 759 p.

BM BN   1577: CSmH ICN MH NcD NN
1579: DLC   1606: ICU

1289   ————.

The Six Bookes of a Commonweale . . . done into English, by Richard Knolles. London, 1606. 794 p.

BM CtY ICN MH NN

1290   Bond, Daniel.
Uncle Sam in Business. Chicago, 1899. 64 p.

DLC NN

1291   Bonfadio, Giuseppe (Josephus Bonfadius), *d.* after 1620.
De Civilis Administrationis Optima Forma. Patavia, 1611. 206 p.

     BN   Bod   DLC

1292   Bonhoure, J.
Dernier État Social, ou Plan d'un Gouvernement Parfait et Invariable. Paris, 1850. 36 p.

     BN

1293   *The Book of the Visions of Zabdeel, the Son of Abdeel. Faithfully Translated from the Original Syriac by an Eminent Traveller, Who Purchas'd the Manuscript at Grand-Cairo.* London, 1743. 39 p.

     ICN

1294   [Bordelon, Laurent], 1653–1730.
Mital, ou Avantures Incroyables. Amsterdam (Paris?), 1708. 438 p.

     BM   BN   CtY   DLC   ICU

1295   Botero, Giovanni, 1540–1617.
Della Ragione di Stato. . . . Con Tre Libri delle Cause della Grandezza a magnificenza della Città. Venice, 1589. 367 p.

     BM   CSmH   CtY   ICU   MH   NcD   1590: BN   ICN   NN
     1601: DLC

1296   —————.
The Cause of the Greatness of Cities. Translated by Thomas Hawkins. London, 1635. 177 p.

     BM   Bod   CtY   ICN   MH

1297   —————.
Della Ragione di Stato . . . . Edited by Carlo Morand. Bologna, 1930.

     DLC   ICN   ICU   NN

1298 ——————.

Delle Relationi Universali di Giovanni Botero Venese. Rome,
1591. 547 p.

1592: BM DLC   1595: BN ICN NN   1596: CtY
1600: CSmH   1622: MH   1630: ICU   1659: NcD

1299 ——————.

Practical Politics. Translated by G. A. Moore. Washington,
D.C. [1949]. 388 p.

DLC ICU MH NcD NN

1300 ——————.

The Reason of State, translated by P. J. and D. P. Waley, and
The Greatness of Cities, translated by Robert Peterson (1606).
New Haven, 1956. 298 p.

BM CSmH CtY DLC ICU MH NcD NN

1301 [Braithwaite, Richard] (Brathwaite), *(pseud.* Castalio Pomerano),
1588–1673.
*Panthalia; or the Royal Romance. A Discourse Stored with
Infinite Variety in Relation to State Government.* London,
1659. 303 p.

BM CSmH CtY ICN MH NN

1302 Brandan, Saint (Saint Brendan), abbot of Clonfert. *Legend.*
(Numerous editions and translations of the 9th c. mss. *Navi-
gatio Brendani.*)

BM BN Bod CSmH CtY DLC ICN ICU MH NcD NN

1303 ——————.

St. Brandan: a Medieval Legend of the Sea. Edited by T.
Wright. London, 1844. 63 p.

BM CSmH CtY ICN ICU MH NcD NN

1304 ——————.

*Les Voyages Merveilleux de Saint Brandan à la Recherche du
Paradis Terrestre.* Edited by Francisque Michel. Paris, 1878.
94 p.

BM BN CtY DLC ICN ICU MH NcD

1305   Brandt, Harry Alonzo, 1885–.
        The Conquest of Peace. Elgin, Ill., 1930. 156 p.

        CtY DLC NN

1306   Brathwaite. *See* Braithwaite, Richard.

1307   Breton, Robert (Robertus Britannus).
        De Optimo Statu Reipublicae. Paris, 1543. 43 p.

        BM BN ICN   1575: MH

1308   Bruce, Stewart E.
        The World in 1931. New York, 1921. 192 p.

        DLC NcD NN

1309   Buckingham, James Silk, 1786–1855.
        National Evils and Practical Remedies, with a Plan for a Model Town. London, 1849. 512 p.

        BM CtY DLC ICU MH NN

1310   Buis, Paul (Paulus Busius), *ca.* 1570–1617.
        . . . *de Republica Libri Tres, Quibus Tota Politicae Ratio Nova et Succincta Methodo Ingenuae Eiusdem Praxi Applicatur.* Franckerae, 1613. 352 p.

        BN ICN

1311   Burman, Pieter the Elder (Petrus Burmannus; Peter Burmanns), 1668–1741.
        Somnium, Sive Iter in Arcadiam Novam Publice Narratum in Majori Academiae Ultrajectinae Acroaterio. Utrecht, 1710.

        BM Bod   1725: CSmH   n.d.: BN

1312   Cabrera, Juan de.
        Crisis Politica; Determina el Mas Florido Imperio, y la Mejor Institucion de Principes, y Ministros. Madrid, 1719. 771 p.

        BM ICU NcD

1313   Caimo, Pompeo (Pompeius Caimus), 1568–1638.
        Parallelo Politico delle Republiche Antiche, e Moderne, in Cui
        Coll' Essame de'Veri Fondamenti de'Governi Civili, si Ante-
        pongono Gli Moderna a Gli Antichi, e la Forma della Republica
        Veneta, a Qualcunque Altra Forma delle Republiche Antiche.
        Padua, 1627. 156 p.

        BM BN DLC ICN ICU

1314   Call, Henry Laurens.
        The Coming Revolution. Boston, 1895. 239 p.

        DLC NN   1896: CtY ICU MH

1315   Campo y Gallardo, Juan de.
        Monarchia Perfecta. Logroño, 1639.

        Bod

1316   *Canary-Birds Naturalized in Utopia, a Canto.* London, *ca.* 1708.
        24 p.

        BM CSmH CtY ICN MH NcD NN

1317   Caraffa, Carlo Maria, 1646–1695.
        Instruccion Christiana de Principes y Reyes. Palermo, 1688.
        391 p.

        BM ICN NcD

1318   Case, John, *d.* 1600.
        Sphaera Civitatis; Hoc Est; Reipublicae Recte Ac Pie Secundum
        Leges Administrandae Ratio. Oxford, 1588. 740 p.

        BM BN MH   1589: NN   1593: ICU   1604: ICN

1319   Casparian, Gregory.
        An Anglo-American Alliance; a Serio-Comic Romance and
        Forecast of the Future. Floral Park, N.Y., 1906. 144 p.

        CtY DLC ICU MH

1320   Caspary, Adolf, 1898–.
        Die Maschinenutopie. Berlin, 1927. 101 p.

        BM MH

1321   [Caswell, Edward Alexis], 1844–1919.
>*Toil and Self, by Myself and Another.* Chicago and New York, 1900. 154 p.

>DLC NN

1322   Cavalcanti, Bartolommeo, 1503–1562.
>*Trattati Overo Discorsi di M. Bartolomeo Cavalcanti Sopra gli Ottimi Reggimenti delle Republiche Antiche et Moderne.* Venice, 1571. 77 p.

>BM BN CtY DLC ICN ICU NcD   1805: MH NN

1323   Cetti, Carlo.
>*Tre Dialoghi.* Como, 1933. 135 p.

>BM BN NN

1324   [Chamberlen, Peter], 1601–1683.
>*The Poore Mans Advocate, or, Englands Samaritan. Powring Oyle and Wyne into the Wounds of the Nation.* London, 1649. 46 p.

>BM CSmH CtY MH

1325   *Chaos; or, a Discourse, Wherein is Presented . . . a Frame of Government by Way of a Republique . . . By a Well-Willer to the Publique Weal.* London, 1659. 54 p.

>BM CSmH ICU MH

1326   Chelidonius Tigurinus (*pseud.*). *See* Boaistuau de Launay, Pierre.

1327   Churchill, A. T.
>*The New Industrial Dawn.* Seattle, 1939. 124 p.

>DLC NcD NN

1328   Churchill, Reginald Charles.
>*A Short History of the Future . . . Based on the Most Reliable Authorities.* London, 1955. 192 p.

>Bod DLC ICN MH NcD

1329   Ciofro (*pseud.*). *See* Bandelloni, Cesare Emilio.

1330   Clauzel, Raymond, 1871–.
L'Île des Femmes; Roman. Paris, 1922. 271 p.

BN DLC NN

1331   ——————.
L'Île des Hommes; Roman. Paris, 1924. 243 p.

BN DLC NN

1332   Collens, Thomas Wharton, 1812–1879.
The Eden of Labor; or, The Christian Utopia. Philadelphia, 1876. 228 p.

BM CSmH CtY DLC ICN ICU MH NN

1333   Collier, John, 1901–.
Tom's a-Cold. A Tale. London, 1933. 320 p.

BM DLC MH NcD NN

1334   [Collin de Plancy, Jacques Albin Simon] (*pseuds.* M. Hormisdas-Peath; M. Jacques St. Albin), 1794–1881.
Voyage au Centre de la Terre . . . au Pôle Nord et dans des Pays Inconnus, Traduit de l'Anglais de M. Hormisdas-Peath, par M. Jacques de St. Albin. 3 vols. Paris, 1821.

BN   1823: BM

1335   Colvin, Ian Goodhope, 1912–.
Domesday Village. London, 1948. 126 p.

BM NcD NN

1336   Comenius, Johann Amos (Jan Amos Komensky), 1592–1670.
The Labyrinth of the World and the Paradise of the Heart. Translated by Count Lützow. London, 1901 (written in 1623). 271 p.

BM CSmH CtY DLC ICN ICU MH NN

1337   Considérant, Victor Prosper, 1808–1893.
Destinée Sociale. 3 vols. Paris, 1837.

BM BN CtY DLC ICN ICU MH NcD NN
1848: CSmH

1338 ———.

The Difficulty Solved, or the Government of the People by Themselves. Liverpool, 1851. 80 p.

BM

1339 Contarini, Gasparo, cardinal, 1484–1542.
De Magistratibus et Republica Venetorum. Paris, 1543. 115 p.

BN ICN ICU   1544: CtY NN   1545: NcD
1547: MH   1551: DLC   1589: BM CSmH

1340 ———.

The Commonwealth and Government of Venice. Translated by Lewis Lewkenor. London, 1599. 230 p.

BM CSmH CtY DLC ICN MH NcD NN

1341 Contarini, Pietro Maria, d. 1610.
Compendio Universal di Republica. Venice, 1602. 280 p.

BM BN Bod

1342 Cornelison, Peter (pseud.). See Plockhoy, Pieter Cornelis.

1343 Cornelius, Peter (pseud.). See Plockhoy, Pieter Cornelis.

1344 Cremonensis, Marcus Hieronymus Vida. See Vida, Marco Girolamo.

1345 Crucé, Éméric (Éméric; Emericus Crucejus; Emery de la Croix), 1590–1648.
Le Nouveau Cynée, ou Discours d'Éstat Représentant les Occasions et Moyens d'Establir une Paix Généralle, et la Liberté du Commerce par Toute le Monde. Paris, 1623. 226 p.

BN MH

1346 ———.

The New Cyneas. Edited by T. W. Balch. Philadelphia, 1909. 363 p.

BM CtY DLC ICU MH NcD NN

1347   Crusoe, Robinson (*pseud.*).
       Looking Upwards: or, Nothing New by Robinson Crusoe.
       Auckland, 1892. 35 p.

       BM

1348   Daudet, Alphonse, 1840–1897.
       Port-Tarascon; Dernières Aventures de l'Illustre Tartarin. Paris,
       1890. 392 p.

       BM BN CtY DLC ICU MH NcD NN   1930: ICN

1349   ——————.
       Port Tarascon; the Last Adventures of the Illustrious Tartarin.
       Translated by Henry James. New York, 1891. 359 p.

       BM CSmH CtY DLC ICN ICU MH NcD NN

1350   Denturk, Henry Cornelis, 1880–.
       Vision of a State of Rightness on a Spiritual Foundation, a
       Short Outline of Government Whereby all Men Have the
       Same Rights and Privileges with the Capitalistic System Abol-
       ished. Huntington, N.Y., 1940. 22 p.

       DLC NN

1351   *Discours de Jacophile du Japon . . . sur le Voyage . . . à Aretipolis*
       . . . Tire du Cabinet de Monsieur de Savignac en Sa Maison
       d'Orador. N.p.., 1605. 194 p.

       BN

1352   Donato, Nicolò, 1705–1765.
       L'Uomo di Governo. Verona, 1753. 445 p.

       ICN

1353   ——————.
       L'Homme d'État. 3 vols. Liege, 1767.

       BM BN ICN ICU MH NcD

1354   ——————.
       L'Hombre de Estado. 3 vols. Madrid, 1789–91.

       NcD

1355   Donnelly, Ignatius, 1831–1901.
        Atlantis, the Antediluvian World. New York, 1882. 490 p.

        BM BN CSmH CtY DLC ICN ICU MH NcD
        1910: NN

1356   ————.
        Atlantis, the Antediluvian World. Edited by Egerton Sykes.
        New York, 1949. 355 p.

        BM DLC ICN MH NcD NN

1357   ————.
        Ragnarok: the Age of Fire and Gravel. New York, 1883. 452 p.

        BM BN CSmH CtY DLC ICN NcD NN

1358   ————.
        The Golden Bottle. New York and St. Paul, 1892. 313 p.

        BM CSmH CtY DLC ICN ICU NcD NN

1359   Dornau, Caspar (Caspar Dornaius), 1577–1632.
        Charidemus, Hoc Est de Morum Pulchritudine, Necessitate,
        Utilitate, ad Civilem Conversationem, Oratio Auspicalis, Habita
        in Illustri Panegyre Gymnasi Schönaichi ad Oderam. Witten-
        berg, 1617. 51 p.

        BM CtY

1360   [Dornkrell, Jakob (Jacobus Dorncreilus)] (*pseud*. Cordesius a
        Verimunt), *fl*. 1643.
        Politia Vere Beata Imo Beatissima: die Aller Vollkommnestund
        Glücksäligste Regiments-Verfassung der Ganzen Welt, Ent-
        decket durch Treuhertz von Wahrmund. Danzig, 1700.

        Bäyrische Staatsbibliothek, Munich

1361   Dorrington, Edward (*pseud*.). *See* Longueville, Peter.

1362   Dudley, Edmund, 1462(?)–1510.
        The Tree of the Commonwealth. Manchester, 1859. 66 p.
        (Written 1509–10 in the Tower of London.)

        BM CSmH CtY DLC ICN ICU MH NN

1363   ————.
The Tree of Commonwealth. Edited by D. M. Brodie. Cambridge, 1948. 111 p.

BM BN CSmH CtY DLC ICN ICU MH NcD NN

1364   [Dufresny, Charles, sieur de la Rivière], 1654–1724.
Amusements sérieux et comiques. Paris, 1699. 288 p.

BM BN DLC MH   1700: ICU   1701: CtY NN
1719: CSmH ICN   1921: NcD

1365   [Dulaurens, Henri Joseph], 1719–1797.
Le Compere Mathieu; ou les Bigarrures de l'Espirit Humain. 2 vols. London, 1766.

ICN   1722: BM DLC   1777: BN Bod NcD
1787: ICU   1792: MH   1793: CtY   1801: NN

1366   Dunham, David (*pseud.*). *See* Smith, David Eugene.

1367   D'Urfey, Thomas, 1653–1723.
A Common-Wealth of Women; a Play. London, 1686. 55 p.

BM CSmH CtY DLC ICN ICU MH NcD

1368   ————.
Wonders in the Sun; or, the Kingdom of the Birds, (a Comick Opera). London, 1706. 69 p.

BM CSmH DLC ICN ICU MH NN   1964: NcD

1369   Eliot, Sir John, 1592–1632.
The Monarchie of Man. Edited by Alexander Grosart. 2 vols. London, 1879. (Written *ca.* 1631.)

BM CSmH CtY DLC ICN ICU MH NN

1370   Éméric. *See* Crucé, Éméric.

1371   Erizzo, Sebastiano, 1525–1585.
Le Sei Giornate. Venice, 1567. 93 p.

BM CSmH CtY ICN MH NcD   1667: BN
1794: DLC   1805: NN

1372 —————.

    "Le Sei Giornate." In *Novellieri Minori del Cinquecento,* edited by G. Gigli and F. Nicolini, pp. 203–429. Bari, 1912.

    BM CSmH CtY ICN MH NcD NN

1373 —————.

    Discorso de i Governi Civili. Venice, 1570. 14 p.

    BM DLC ICN ICU NcD   1501: BN ICU MH

1374 Erythraeus. *See* Rossi, Giovanni Vittorio.

1375 Everett, Henry Lexington.
    The People's Program; the Twentieth Century Is Theirs. New York, 1892. 213 p.

    CSmH DLC ICN ICU MH

1376 Fairfield, Charles.
    The Socialist Revolution of 1888, by an Eye Witness. London, 1884. 35 p.

    BM

1377 Fénelon, François de Salignac de la Mothe, 1651–1715.
    Directions pour la Conscience des Rois et Princes Souverains, Composées pour l'Instruction de Louis de France, duc de Bourgogne . . . Pour Servir de Supplement au Télémaque. The Hague, 1747. 68 p. (First published in 1734 edition of *Avantures de Télémaque* from which it was later suppressed.)

    BM BN DLC MH NcD   1748: NN

1378 —————.

    Proper Heads of Self-Examination for a King. Dublin, 1747. 244 p.

    BM BN DLC ICN NcD

1379 Ferrarius, Johannes Montanus, 1485(?)–1558.
    De Republica Bene Instituenda, Paraenesis; in Qua Tam Pri-

vati, Quam Qui Aliis Praesunt, Officii Sui Non sine Pietatis Studio Praestandi, Secus atque a Philosophis Traditum Sit, Monetur. Basle, 1556. 178 p.

ICN

1380 ——————.

A Woorke of Joannes Ferrarius Montanus Touchynge the Good Orderynge of a Common Weale. Englished by W. Bavande. London, 1559.

BM CSmH DLC ICU

1381 Figueroa. *See* Suárez de Figueroa, Christóbal.

1382 Filippe, Bartholomeu (Bartolomeo Felippe), *d.* 1590.
Tractado del Consejo y de los Consejeros de los Principes. Coimbra, 1584. 146 ff.

BM BN Bod ICN MH NcD

1383 ——————.
The Counseller: a Treatise of Counsels and Counsellers of Princes. Englished by I. T[horius]. London, 1589. 191 p.

BM Bod DLC MH

1384 Firmanius, Pietrus. *See* Zacharie de Lisieux.

1385 Flammerion, Camille, 1842–1925.
Recits de l'Infini. Lumen. Paris, 1873. 415 p.

BM BN   18–: MH   1897: CtY   191–: DLC ICU

1386 ——————.
Lumen. Translated by A. A. M. and R. M. New York, 1897. 223 p.

BM DLC NcD NN

1387 Fontaines, Louis. *See* Zacherie de Lisieux.

1388 Frachetta, Girolamo, 1558–1620.
L'Idea del Libro de'Governi di Stato et di Guerra. Venice, 1592. 63 ff.

BN Bod DLC ICN

1389   ——————.

Il Prencipe . . . nel Quale si Considera il Prencipe et Quanto al Governo dello State et Quanto al Maneggio della Guerra. Rome, 1597. 349 p.

ICN MH   1599: BM BN CtY

1390   ——————.

Il Seminario de'Governi di Stato e di Guerra. Venice, 1613. 795 p.

BN   1617: BM DLC ICU

1391   [Frankenstein, Ernst] (*pseud.* Frank E. Warner), 1881–.
Future of Man; a Study in Human Possibilities. Translated from the Original Manuscript by S. L. Salzedo. London, 1944. 179 p.

BM DLC MH NN

1392   Furió Ceriol, Fadrique, 1532–1592.
El Concejo y Consejeros del Principe. Antwerp, 1559. 83 ff. (Numerous editions and translations.)

BM BN ICU   1560: ICN   1563: MH   1799: NN
1855: NcD

1393   ——————.

El Concejo y Consejeros del Principe. Edited by D. S. Andres. Valencia, 1952. 203 p.

DLC ICN MH NN

1394   ——————.

A Very Briefe and Profitable Treatise Declaring Howe Many Counsells, and What Manner of Counselers a Prince That Will Governe Well Ought to Have. Translated by Thomas Blundevill. London, 1570. 62 leaves.

BM CSmH CtY ICN

1395   ——————.

Of Councils and Counselors (1570) by Thomas Blundeville. (Facsimile.) Edited by Karl-Ludwig Selig. Gainesville, Fla., 1963. 140 p.

BM Bod CSmH CtY DLC ICU MH NcD NN

1396   Gambaruti, Tiberio, *ca.* 1571–1623.
        Discorsi et Osservationi Politiche. Rome, 1612. 363 p.

        BM BN DLC

1397   Ganivet, Angel, 1865–1898.
        Idearium Español. Granada, 1897. 163 p.

        BM NcD   1905: CtY MH   1928: DLC

1398   [Gentillet, Innocent], *ca.* 1535–*ca.* 1595.
        Discours, sur les Moyens de Bien Gouverner & Maintenir en Bonne Paix un Royaume, ou Autre Principauté. Geneva, 1576. 639 p.

        BM BN CSmH CtY ICN MH NN   1577: NcD
        1579: DLC

1399   [————].
        Commentariorum de Regno aut Quoris Principatu Recte . . . Adversus Nicolaum Machiavellum. N.p., 1577; Leyden, 1647. 708 p.

        BN   1578: ICN MH   1590: Bod
        1647: CSmH DLC ICU

1400   [————].
        A Discourse upon the Meanes of Well Governing and Maintaining in Good Peace, a Kingdome, or Other Principalitie. Translated by Simon Patericke. London, 1602. 374 p.

        BM CSmH CtY DLC ICN ICU MH NcD   1608: NN

1401   Gilman, Bradley, 1857–1932.
        Back to the Soil; or, from Tenement to Farm Colony; a Circular Solution of an Angular Problem. Boston, 1901. 242 p.

        CtY DLC MH NcD NN

1402   Glanvill, Joseph, 1636–1680.
        "Anti-Fanatical Religion, and Free Philosophy. In a Continuation of the New Atlantis." In *Essays on Several Important Subjects in Philosophy and Religion,* essay 7. London, 1676.

        BM BN CSmH CtY DLC ICN ICU MH

[Mss. 62 p. folio, *ca.* 1675, University of Chicago. On revisions of original manuscript, see Jackson I. Cope, "The Cupri-Cosmits: Glanvill on Latitudinarian Anti-Enthusiasm," in *The Huntington Quarterly,* vol. 17, no. 3 (May 1954), pp. 269–86.]

1403   Góslicki, Wawrzyviec (Laurentius Grimalius; Lawrence Gosliski; Lorenzo Grimaldo), 1535–1607.
De Optimo Senatore. In Quibus Magistratuum Officia, Civium Vita Beata, Rerumpub. Foelicitas Explicantur. Venice, 1568. 83 p.
BM BN CtY ICN   1593: MH

1404   ————.
The Counsellor. Exactly Pourtraited in Two Bookes. London, 1598. 155 p.
BM CSmH CtY

1405   ————.
A Common-Wealth of Good Counsaile. Or, Policies Chiefe Counseller. London, 1607. 155 p.
BM

1406   ————.
The Sage Senator Delineated. By J. G. Gent. London, 1660.
ICN

1407   ————.
The Accomplished Senator. By Mr. Oldisworth. London, 1733. 330 p.
BM CSmH DLC ICN MH

1408   [Graffigny, Mme. Françoise d'Issembourg d'Happoncourt], 1695–1758.
Lettres d'une Péruvienne. Paris, 1747. 337 p.
BM BN CtY ICN ICU MH NcD NN   1756: DLC

1409   [————].
Lettres d'une Péruvienne [Augmentées de Celles du Chevalier De'terville]. Amsterdam, 1755. 240 p.
BM BN DLC   1756: CtY DLC   1763: NN

1410   [————].
        Letters of a Peruvian Princess. Translated by P. Durand. 2 vols.
        Paris, 1802.

        BN CSmH DLC NcD NN

1411   Griggs, Sutton Elbert.
        Imperium in Imperio. Cincinnati, 1889. 265 p.

        DLC   1969: CtY ICU MH NcD NN

1412   Grimalius, Laurentius. *See* Góslicki, Wawrzyviec.

1413   Gualandi, Giovanni Bernardo, *d. ca.* 1570.
        De Optimo Principe Dialogus. Florence, 1561.

        ICN

1414   Guerineau de Saint-Péravi, Jean Nicolas Marcellin, 1735–1789.
        *L'Optique; ou le Chinois à Memphis: Essais Traduits de
        l'Egyptienne.* 2 vols. London, 1763.

        BM BN ICU

1415   Haller, Albrecht von, baron, 1708–1777.
        Die Alpen. Bern, 1732. 70 p.

        1795: CtY MH   1795 (French): BN   1959: NcD
        Works: BM DLC NN

1416   ————.
        "Die Alpen." In *Vorboten der Bürgerlichen Kultur,* edited by
        Fritz Brüggemann. Leipzig, 1931.

        BN CtY DLC ICN ICU MH NcD

1417   ————.
        "Die Alpen." In *Vorboten der Bürgerlichen Kultur,* edited by
        H. T. Betteridge. Berlin, 1959. 70 p.

        BN CtY DLC MH NcD NN

1418   [Haller, baron Albrecht von], 1708–1777.
        Usong; eine Morgenländische Geschichte. Bern, 1771. 420 p.

        BM BN CtY NN   1771: MH   1778: BN ICU

1419 [————].
　　　Usong, an Oriental History in Four Books. London, 1773. 316 p.
　　　CtY ICN

1420 [————].
　　　Usong. An Eastern Narrative. Translated by J. Planta. 2 vols.
　　　London, 1772.
　　　CtY ICU

1421 Hamilton, William (*pseud.*). *See* Head, Richard.

1422 [Hare, John], *fl.* 1642–1648.
　　　*Plaine English to Our Wilfull Bearers with Normanisme, or
　　　Some Queries Propounded to and Concerning the Neglectours
　　　of Englands Grand Grievance and Complaint.* London, 1647.
　　　BM CSmH CtY ICN

1423 [————].
　　　*England's Proper and Onely Way to an Establishment in Hon-
　　　our, Freedome, Peace and Happinesse: or, the Norman Yoke
　　　Once More Uncased.* London, 1648. 11 p.
　　　BM CSmH CtY ICN MH

1424 [————].
　　　"England's Proper and Onely Way. . . ." In *The Harleian Mis-
　　　cellany,* 6:175–81. London, 1810.
　　　BM CtY DLC ICN MH NcD

1425 Hatchett, William (*pseud.*). *See* Bignon, Jean Paul.

1426 [Head, Richard] (*pseud.* William Hamilton), 1637(?)–1686(?).
　　　*O-Brazile, or the Inchanted Island: Being a Perfect Relation of
　　　the Late Discovery and Wonderful Dis-inchantment of an Is-
　　　land on the North of Ireland: with an Account of the Riches
　　　and Commodities Thereof.* London, 1660.
　　　1675: BM Bod CSmH

1427 [————].
　　　The Western Wonder; or, O Brazeel, an Inchanted Island Dis-

covered. . . . *To Which is Added, a Description of a Place, Called, Montecapernia, Relating the Nature of the People, Their Qualities, Humours, etc.* London, 1674. 40 p.

BM ICN MH NN

1428 Heinse, Johann Jakob Wilhelm, 1749–1803.
Ardinghello und die Glückseeligen Inseln. 2 vols. Lemgo, 1787.

CtY MH   1792: ICU   1886: NN   1921: NcD

1429 Heumann, Christoph August, 1681–1764.
Poecile Sive Epistolae Miscellaneae ad Literatissimos Aevi Nostri Viros. 3 vols. Halle, 1722–32.

BM BN ICN ICU MH

1430 Hodge, T. Shirby (*pseud.*). *See* Tracy, Roger Sherman.

1431 [Holbach, Paul Henri Thiry, baron d'], 1723–1789. (Sometimes catalogued Meslier, Jean.)
Le Bon Sens, ou, Idées Naturelles Opposées aux Idées Surnaturelles. London, 1772. 266 p.

BM BN MH NN   1774: ICU   1792: NcD   1834: NN

1432 [————].
Good Sense. Edited by N. T. London, 1826. 170 p.

BM CSmH ICN   1830: CtY   1831: MH

1433 Hormisdas-Peath, M. (*pseud.*). *See* Collin de Plancy, Jacques.

1434 [Horner, Jacob W.] (*pseud.* Dr. Walter H. Sensney).
Military Socialism. Indianapolis, 1911. 109 p.

DLC

1435 Hume, David, 1711–1776.
"Idea of a Perfect Commonwealth." In *Essays, Moral and Political,* 1:505–23. Edinburgh, 1741–42.

BM CSmH CtY ICN MH   1748: DLC ICU NcD
1875: NN

1436   Hutchinson, Alfred L., 1859–.
       The Limit of Wealth. New York, 1907. 285 p.
       BM CtY DLC ICU MH NcD NN

1437   Ingelo, Nathaniel, 1621(?)–1683.
       Bentivolio and Urania. London, 1660. 283 p.
       BM CSmH CtY MH   1669: ICN ICU NN
       1673: BN NcD

1438   [Juan de Santa Maria], *d.* 1622.
       Tratado de Republica, y Policia Christiana. Para Reyes y Principes: para los que en el Govierno Tienen Sus Vezes. Madrid, 1615. 407 p.
       ICN   1617: BN   1621: BM DLC

1439   [————].
       Christian Policie: or, the Christian Common-wealth. Translated by Edward Blount. London, 1632. 481 p.
       BM CSmH NN   1634: CtY

1440   [————].
       Policy Unveiled; or, Maximes of State. London, 1650. 481 p.
       DLC NcD

1441   *The King of Utopia His Letter to the Citizens of Cosmopolis, the Metropolitan City of Utopia. Printed at Cosmopolis in the Year 7461.* London, 1647.
       Bod

1442   Kirkby, John, 1705–1754.
       The Capacity and Extent of the Human Understanding; Exemplified in the Extraordinary Case of Automathes; a Young Nobleman, Who Was Accidentally Left in His Infancy, upon a

Desolate Island, and Continued Nineteen Years in That Solitary State. London, 1745. 284 p. (Taken without acknowledgment from an earlier anonymous work.)

BM CtY ICN MH   1747: NcD   1761: CSmH
1812: BN

1443   Koepsel, Louis Herman, 1864–.
        A Prophecy: The Human Community; or, The True Social Order. San Francisco, 1919. 121 p.

        CtY NN

1444   Komensky, Jan Amos. *See* Comenius, Johann Amos.

1445   Kruse, Louis Frederick Vinding, 1880–.
        Det Kommende Samfund. 2 vols. Copenhagen, 1944.

        DLC NcD

1446   ————.
        The Community of the Future. Translated by I. Lund and others. London, 1950. 828 p.

        CtY DLC ICU NcD   1952: MH NN

1447   Lahontan, Louis Armand de Lom d'Arce, baron de, 1666–1715.
        Nouveaux Voyages de M. le Baron de Lahontan dans l'Amerique Septentrionale. 2 vols. The Hague, 1703.

        BM BN CSmH CtY DLC ICN ICU MH NN

1448   ————.
        New Voyages to North America. 2 vols. London, 1703.

        BM CtY DLC ICN MH NcD NN   1905: CSmH ICU

1449   Lamennais, Hugues Félicité Robert de, 1782–1854.
        L'Avenir. Paris, 1830–31.

        BN

1450   La Mettrie, Julien Offray de (Offray de la Mettrie), 1709–1751.
       L'Homme Machine. Leyde, 1748. 148 p.

       BN Bod CtY DLC MH   1865: NcD   1921: NN
       1960: ICN

1451   ——————.
       Man a Machine. London, 1749.

       MH NN   1750: BM Bod ICN   1912: CtY ICU

1452   Landino, Cristoforo, 1424–1504.
       Commento sopra la Comedia di Dante [*in*] *Dante Alighieri, La
       Divina Commedia.* Florence, 1481.

       BM BN Bod CSmH ICN   1491: DLC MH NN
       1493: NcD   1536: ICU

1453   La Perrière, Guillaume de, 1499–1565.
       Le Miroir Politique. Lyons, 1555. 199 p.

       BM BN MH   1567: DLC ICN

1454   ——————.
       The Mirrour of Policie. London, 1598. 284 p.

       BM CSmH CtY MH NN   1599: DLC ICN

1455   ——————.
       *Theo-Politica, or a Body of Divinity Containing the Rules of
       the Special Providence of God.* London, 1659.

       MH   1705: CtY

1456   La Place, Pierre de, 1520–1572 (probable author).
       *Discours Politiques sur la Roye d'Entrer Deûement aux Éstats,
       et Manière de Constamment s'y Maintenir et Gouverner.* Paris,
       1574. 114 p.

       BM ICN MH

1457   Lemieux, Pierre.
       *Universalism, the New Spirit, a Reborn World, Earthly Happi-
       ness, the Ideal State!!!* Montreal, 1934. 215 p.

       DLC NN

1458   [Le Moyne, Nicolas René Desiré] (*pseud.* Médius), 1796–1875.
Doctrine Hiérarchique Fusionnaire: Construction d'une Société Véridique—Juste—Affective—et Libre. Metz, 1860. 352 p.

BM BN ICN NcD

1459   Lesczinski. *See* Stanislaus I.

1460   L'Estrange, Miles (*pseud.?*).
What We Are Coming To. (A Forecast.) Edinburgh, 1892. 124 p.

BM

1461   Lom d'Arce, Louis Armand, baron de Lahontan. *See* Lahontan, Louis Armand de Lom d'Arce.

1462   [Longueville, Peter] (*pseud.* Edward Dorrington).
The Hermit: or, the Unparalled Sufferings and Surprising Adventures of Mr. Philip Quarll, an Englishman. Westminster, 1727. 264 p.

BM CSmH CtY ICN MH   1746: ICU NN
1795: DLC NcD

1463   Low, Archibald Montgomery, 1888–.
The Future. London and New York, 1925. 203 p.

BM DLC NcD

1464   Lubin, David, 1849–1919.
Let There Be Light. New York and London, 1900. 526 p.

BM CSmH CtY DLC ICU NcD NN

1465   Mably, Gabriel Bonnot de, abbé, 1709–1785.
Entretiens de Phocion, sur la Rapport de la Morale avec la Politique; Traduits du Grec de Nicoclès avec des Remarques. Amsterdam, 1763. 249 p.

BM BN DLC ICN   1767: NcD NN   1789: CtY
1795: ICU   Works: MH

1466 ————.

Phocion's Conversations: or, the Relation between Morality and Politics. Edited by W. Macbeam. London, 1769. 303 p.

BM DLC   Works: MH

1467 ————.

Des Droits et des Devoirs du Citoyen. Kell, 1789. 367 p.

BM BN CtY DLC NcD NN   Works: ICU MH

1468 McCutcheon, Duval.
America Made Young; a Plan for a More Perfect Society. Philadelphia, 1932. 195 p.

DLC

1469 Madeleine, Jean de la, seigneur de Chevremont.
Discours de l'Éstat et Office d'un Bon Roy, Prince ou Monarque. Paris, 1575. 79 p.

BM BN

1470 Mahistre, Henri.
La France de Demain: Solutions Économiques, Politiques et Sociales. Paris, 1903. 131 p.

DLC MH

1471 [Mailhol, Gabriel], 1725–1791.
Les Bonnets, ou Talemik et Zinéra, Histoire Moderne. Traduite de l'Arabe. London, 1765. 174 p.

BN ICN

1472 Martin, Frederick Townsend, 1849–1914.
The Passing of the Idle Rich. New York, 1911. 263 p.

BM CSmH CtY DLC ICU MH NcD NN

1473 [Maubert de Gouvest, Jean Henri], 1721–1767.
Lettres Iroquoises. 2 vols. in 1. Irocopolis (Lausanne?), 1752.

BM BN CtY DLC ICN NcD NN   1755: MH

1474   [————].
      Lettres Chérakéesiennes. Rome, 1769. 168 p.

      BN ICN MH

1475   [————].
      Lettres Chérakéesiennes. Edited by Enea Balmas. Paris, 1962.
      250 p.

      BN ICU NcD NN

1476   Médius (*pseud.*). *See* Le Moyne, Nicolas René Desiré.

1477   Meier-Lutz, H.
      Geldlose Zukunft. Einzige Lösung der Socialen Frage. Berlin,
      1908. 16 p.

      NN

1478   Mejia. *See* Mexia, Pedro.

1479   Melville, Herman, 1819–1891.
      Mardi, and a Voyage Thither. 2 vols. New York, 1849.

      BM CtY DLC ICN ICU MH NN   1923: NcD

1480   Memmo, Giovanni Maria, *d.* 1553.
      *Dialogo . . . nel Quale Dopo Alcune Filosofiche Dispute, si
      Forma un Perfetto Prencipe, & una Perfetta Republica.* Venice,
      1563. 194 p.

      BM BN CSmH DLC ICN

1481   Mendo, Andres, 1608–1685.
      *Principe Perfecto y Ministros Ajustados, Documentos Politicos,
      y Morales, en Emblemas.* Salamanca, 1657. 409 p.

      1662: BM BN DLC ICN NN   1816: NcD

1482   Merbury, Charles, *fl.* 1581.
      *A Briefe Discourse of Royall Monarchie, as of the Best Com-
      mon Weale: Wherein the Suject May Beholde the Sacred
      Majestie of the Princes Most Royall Estate.* London, 1581. 52 p.

      BM CSmH ICU MH

1483   Meslier, Jean. *See* Holbach, Paul Henri Thiry, baron d'.

1484   Mexia, Pedro (Mejia), 1496–1552.
        Silva de Varia Leccion. Seville, 1540. 288 ff. (Numerous editions and translations.)

        Biblioteca Nacional, Madrid   1544: BM NN   1550: BN
        1553: ICU MH   1587: CtY   1662: ICN   1673: NcD

        [See also *Treasurie* . . . .]

1485   Mills, Walter Thomas, 1856–.
        The Struggle for Existence. Chicago, 1904. 635 p.

        BM CSmH CtY DLC ICN NN

1486   Molinier, Étienne, *d.* 1650.
        Les Politiques Chrestiennes, ou Tableau des Vertus Politique Considérées en l'Éstat Chrestien. Paris, 1621. 506 p.

        BN

1487   —————.
        A Mirrour for Christian States; or, a Table of Politick Vertues Considerable amongst Christians . . . Translated into English, by William Tyrwhit. London, 1635. 361 p.

        BM Bod CSmH ICN MH NN

1488   Montpensier, Anne Marie Louise Henriette d'Orleans, duchesse de, 1627–1693.
        La Relation de l'Îsle Imaginaire, et l'Histoire de la Princesse de Paphlagonie. N.p. (Bordeaux?), 1659. 166 p.

        BM BN   1723: MH   1805: DLC

1489   Morelly, abbé.
        Code de la Nature, ou, le Véritable Esprit de ses Loix de Tout Temps Négligé ou Méconnu. Par-tout, Chez le Vrai Sage, 1755. 240 p.

        BM BN   1757: ICU NcD   1760: CtY ICN
        1841: NN

1490   ————.
    Code de la Nature. . . . Edited by Édouard Dolléans. Paris, 1910. 119 p.
    BM BN CtY DLC ICU MH NN

1491   Moréri, Louis, 1643–1680.
    Le Pays d'Amour, Nouvelle Allégorique. Lyons, 1665. 86 p.
    BN

1492   Muratori, Lodovico Antonio, 1672–1750.
    Della Pubblica Felicità, Oggetto de'Buoni Principi Trattato. Lucca, 1749. 460 p.
    BM ICN MH NcD   n.d.: DLC

1493   ————.
    Traité sur le Bonheur Public. Translated by L. P. D. L. B[arnabite]. 2 vols. Lyons, 1772.
    BM BN NcD

1494   ————.
    La Publica Felicidad, Objeto de los Buenos Principes. Madrid, 1790. 392 p.
    NcD   Works: ICU

1495   Murry, John Middleton, 1889–1957.
    Things to Come. London, 1928. 318 p.
    BM CtY DLC ICU MH NcD NN

1496   [Nedham, Marchamount], 1620–1678.
    The Excellencie of a Free State: or, the Right Constitution of a Commonwealth. London, 1656. 246 p.
    BM CSmH CtY ICN MH   1790 (French): BN

1497   [————].
    The Excellencie of a Free State. . . . Edited by Richard Barton. London, 1767. 176 p.
    BM Bod CtY DLC ICU MH

1498   Nemo, Omen (*pseud.*). *See* Rehm, Warren S.

1499   Neuville, T.
       Voyage du Sens Commun a l'Isle d'Utopie. Dijon, 1866. 24 p.
       BN

1500   Niemann, August (Wilhelm Otto August), 1839–1919.
       Der Weltkrieg, Deutsche Träume; Roman. Berlin, 1904. 386 p.
       BM BN CtY DLC MH NN

1501   [Nordenskiöld, August], 1754–1792.
       Plan for a Free Community upon the Coast of Africa, Under the Protection of Great Britain; but Entirely Independent of All European Laws and Governments. London, 1789. 51 p.
       DLC

1502   Norman, Alfred.
       The Best Is Yet to Be: a Forecast of the Perfect Social State. London, 1935. 138 p.
       BM DLC NN

1503   Norwood, Robert, *fl.* 1651.
       A Pathway unto England's Perfect Settlement; and its Centre and Foundation of Rest and Peace. London, 1653. 61 p.
       BM CSmH DLC NN

1504   *La Nouveau Panurge avec la Navigation en l'Île Imaginaire.* La Rochelle, n.d. (1615?).
       BN

1505   Palmieri, Matteo, 1406–1475.
       Libro della Vita Civile. Florence, 1529. 99 ff.
       BM BN CSmH CtY DLC ICN ICU MH NcD NN

1506   ————.
       Libro della Vita Civile. Edited by Felice Battaglia. Bologna, 1944.
       ICN ICU

1507   Paruta, Paolo, 1540–1598.
        Della Perfettione della Vita Politica. Venice, 1579. 316 p.

        BM BN MH NcD NN   1599: ICU
        1852: CtY DLC ICN

1508   ————.
        *Discorsi Politici . . . ne i Quáli si Considerano Diversi Fatti
        Illustri, e Memorabili di Principi, e di Republiche Antiche e
        Moderne.* Venice, 1599. 636 p.

        BM BN CSmH CtY DLC ICN MH NcD NN
        1629: ICU   1827: DLC

1509   ————.
        Discorsi Politici. . . . Edited by Giorgio Candeloro. Bologna,
        1943. 386 p.

        CtY DLC ICN NcD

1510   ————.
        *Politick Discourses . . . Whereunto is Added, a Short Soliloquy
        . . . Rendered into English by the Right Honorable, Henry Earl
        of Monmouth.* London, 1657. 203 p.

        BM CSmH CtY ICN ICU

1511   Pataud, Émile and Émile Pouget.
        Comment Nous Ferons la Révolution. Paris, 1909. 298 p.

        BM BN DLC ICN MH   1911: NcD

1512   ————.
        *Syndicalism and the Co-operative Commonwealth. How We
        Shall Bring About the Revolution.* Translated by C. and F.
        Charles. Oxford, 1913. 270 p.

        BM CtY DLC ICU MH NcD NN

1513   [Patrizi, Francesco], bishop (Patritius), 1413–1494.
        De Institutione Reip. Paris, 1535. 131 ff.

        BN ICN   1552: CtY   1578: NN   1594: BM MH
        1610: DLC

1514 [————].

A Moral Methode of Civile Policie. Contayninge a Learned and Fruictful Discourse of the Institution, State and Government of a Common Weale. Abridged oute of the Commentaries of . . . F. Patricius. Done oute of Latine into Englishe by R. Robinson. London, 1576.

BM CSmH CtY MH

1515 [————].

. . . de Regno et Regis Institutione. Paris, 1519. 60 p.

BN DLC   1531: ICN NcD   1552: CtY   1567: BM NN 1594: MH

1516 Perrot d'Ablancourt, Nicholas, 1606–1664.

Lucien de la Traduction de N. Perrot Sr. d'Ablancourt. 2 vols. Paris, 1654.

BM BN CtY   1660: NN   1664: ICU   1670: NcD 1688: ICN

1517 Pettitt, Edward, 1654–1709.

The Visions of Government, Wherein the Antimonarchical Principles and Practices of All Fanatical Commonwealths-Men and Jesuitical Politicians are Discovered, Confuted and Exposed. London, 1684. 248 p.

BM CSmH CtY DLC ICN ICU   1686: NN

1518 Phelps, Corwin.

An Ideal Republic; or, Way Out of the Fog. Chicago, 1896. 403 p.

DLC

1519 Platina, Bartolomeo de'Sacchi, dit Battista, 1421–1481.

De Optimo Cive. Venice, 1504.

BM BN   1530: NcD   Works: ICU

1520 [Plockhoy, Pieter Cornelis] (Cornelison) (pseud. Peter Cornelius), 1620(?)–1700(?).

The Way to the Peace and Settlement of These Nations, Fully

Discovered in Two Letters, Delivered to His Late Highnesse and One to the Present Parliament . . . by Peter Cornelius, van Zurick Zee. London, 1659. 30 p.

BM CSmH DLC ICU MH NcD

1521   [————].
A Way Propounded to Make the Poor in These and Other Nations Happy, By Bringing Together a Fit Suitable and Well Qualified People into One Household-Government, or Little Commonwealth. London, 1659. 34 p.

BM ICN MH NN

1522   [————].
"The Way to the Peace . . . " and "A Way Propounded. . . . " In *Plockhoy from Zurich-Zee,* by Leland and Marvin Harder, pp. 107–73. Mennonite Historical Series, no. 2. Newton, Kan., 1952.

CSmH DLC ICU NcD NN

1523   Pomerano, Castalio (*pseud.*). *See* Braithwaite, Richard.

1524   Postel, Guillaume, 1510–1581.
Les Raisons de la Monarchie. Paris, 1551. 48 p.

BM BN

1525   Pouget, Émile. *See* Pataud, Émile.

1526   Psalmanazar, George, 1679(?)–1763. (The true identity of this French literary imposter is still unknown.)
An Historical and Geographical Description of Formosa (an Island Subject to the Emperor of Japan). Giving an Account of the Religion, Customs, Manners, etc. of the Inhabitants. London, 1704. 331 p.

BM CSmH DLC ICN MH NcD   1705 (French): BN

1527   Quaia, Joannes Genesius (Quaya).
Liber de Civitate Christi. Regii, 1501.

BM

1528   Quarto di Palo, Luigi.
        Principi per la Constituzione della Republica Universale. An-
        dria, 1949. 48 p.
        DLC

1529   [Quesnel, Pierre] (*pseud.* Hercule Rasiel de Selva), 1699–1774.
        *Histoire de l'Admirable Dom Inigo de Guipuscoa, Chevalier de
        la Vierge, et Fondateur de la Monarchie des Inighistes . . . Par
        le Sieur Hercule Rasiel de Selva.* 2 vols. The Hague, 1736.
        BN ICN MH   1738: BM

1530   [————————].
        The History of the Wonderful Don Ignatius de Loyola. 2 vols.
        London, 1754.
        BM   1755: ICN

1531   Rabelais, François, 1494(?)–1553.
        (Original editions in BN; later editions in all other libraries.)
        Gargantua. N.p., n.d. [1532].

1532   ————————.
        Pantagruel. Lyons, 1532.

1533   ————————.
        L'Îsle Sonante. N.p., 1562.

1534   Rasiel de Selva, Hercule (*pseud.*). *See* Quesnel, Pierre.

1535   [Rehm, Warren S.] (*pseud.* Omen Nemo).
        *The Practical City. A Future City Romance; or, a Study in
        Environment.* Lancaster, Penn., 1898. 35 p.
        DLC

1536   [Restif de la Bretonne, Nicolas Edme], 1734–1806.
        *Les Gynographes, ou Idées de Deux Honnêtes Femmes sur un
        Projet de Règlement Proposé à Toute l'Europe.* The Hague,
        1777. 568 p.
        BM BN CtY DLC MH NN   1930: ICN   1931: NcD

1537   [————].

L'Andrographe, ou Idées d'un Honnête Homme Sur un Projet de Règlement Proposé à Toute les Nations de l'Europe. The Hague, 1782. 476 p.

BM BN CtY DLC MH

1538   Richer, Henri, 1685–1748.

Fables Nouvelles, Mises en Vers. Dédiées à Son Altesse Sérénissime Monseigneur Prince de Conty. Paris, 1729. 229 p.

BN NcD   1744: CtY   1748: BM

1539   Ridder, Jan Herman de, 1816–1886.

Een Nederlandsch Deschenk voor den Vorst van Eutopia; eene Voorlezing. Gouda, 1848. 36 p.

Columbia University, New York

1540   [Rossi, Giovanni Vittorio] (Janus Nicius Erythraeus), 1577–1647.

Jani Nicii Erythraei Eudemiae Libri VIII. Leyden, 1637. 311 p.

BM BN   1645: MH

1541   [Rouillé d'Orfeuil, Auguste.]

L'Alambic des Loix, ou Observations de l'Ami des François sur l'Homme et sur les Loix. Hispaan (i.e., Paris), 1773. 477 p.

BM BN ICN MH

1542   Saavedra Fajardo, Diego de, 1584–1648.

Idea de un Principe Politico Christiano, Representada en Cien Empresas. Monaco, 1640. 711 p. (Numerous editions and translations.)

BN Bod MH NN   1642: BM ICU   1648: ICN
1650: DLC   1655: NcD   1668: CSmH

1543   ————.

Idea de un Principe Politico Christiano.... Edited by Vicento Garciá de Diego. 4 vols. Madrid, 1927–30.

BM ICN ICU MH NcD

1544 ————.
The Royal Politician Represented in One Hundred Emblems. Translated by Sir James Astry. 2 vols. London, 1700.
BM Bod CSmH DLC ICN ICU MH NcD NN

1545 Sagean, Mathieu.
"Découverte du Pays des Acaanibas par Mathieu Sagean et ses Aventures." In *Découvertes et Établissements des Français dans l'Ouest et dans le Sud de l'Amérique Septentrionale (1615–1754)*, by Pierre Margry, 6:95–174. Paris, 1886.
CtY NcD NN

1546 ————.
The Original Manuscript Account of the Kingdom of Acaniba, Given by the Affadavit of Matthew Saigean. London, 1755. 10 p.
BM NN

1547 ————.
"Matthew Sagean and His Adventures." *The Historical Magazine* 10 (March 1866) : 67–71.
CtY NcD NN

1548 St. Albin, M. Jacques (*pseud.*). *See* Collin de Plancy, Jacques.

1549 Saint-Pierre, Jacques Henri Bernardin de, 1737–1814.
L'Arcadie. Angers, 1781. 140 p. (Numerous editions and translations.)
MH   1784: BM   1795: BN NN   1797: DLC
1818: ICN ICU NcD

1550 ————.
Paul et Virginie. Lausanne, 1788. 294 p.
BM MH   1789: BN ICN NcD   1796: DLC
1824: CSmH

1551 ————.
Paul and Virginia. Translated by Helen Maria Williams. Paris, 1795. 274 p.
BM BN ICU NcD NN   1796: CtY DLC MH
1799: BM   1811: ICN

1552   Saint-Thomas, François de.
La Vraye Forme de Bien et Heureusement Régir et Gouverner un Royaume ou Monarchie; Ensemble le Vray Office d'un Bon Prince. Lyons, 1569. 149 p.

BN

1553   Salazar, Juan de, *ca.* 1570(?)–*ca.* 1623(?).
Política Española, Contiene un Discurso Cerca de Su Monarquía, Materias de Estado. Logrono, 1619. 532 p.

BM CtY

1554   ————.
Política Española. . . . Edited by Miguel Herrero García. Madrid, 1945. 287 p.

BM BN CtY DLC ICN MH NcD

1555   Salici, Giovanni Andrea.
Discorsi Politici . . . Utili in Pace, e in Guerra al Reggimento de Prencipe. Sorivoli, 1627. 640 p.

BN ICN NcD

1556   Salveld, Johann Friedrich.
Princeps Christianus et Perfectus. Frankfurt, 1618. 423 p.

NN

1557   Sanders, George A.
Reality: or, Law and Order vs. Anarchy and Socialism. A Reply to Edward Bellamy's Looking Backward and Equality. Cleveland, 1898. 239 p.

BM CtY DLC ICN ICU MH NcD NN

1558   Sandisson, M. de (*pseud.*). *See* Bignon, Jean Paul.

1559   Sannazaro, Jacopo, 1458–1530.
Libro Pastorale Nominato Arcadio. Venice, 1502. 56 leaves.

BM   1504: BN MH   1512: CtY ICN   1514: CSmH
1524: DLC   1531: NcD   1546: NN   1578: ICU

1560   ——————.
> *Libro Pastorale*. . . . Edited by Enrico Carrara. Turin, 1926.
> 157 p.

> CtY DLC ICN ICU NcD

1561   Sansovino, Francesco, 1521–1586.
> *Del Governo de i Regni et Delle Republiche Cosi Antiche Come Moderne.* Venice, 1561. 201 p.

> BM MH NN   1567: BN CSmH CtY ICN ICU
> 1578: NcD   1583: DLC

1562   Scheffer, Johannes Gerhard (Joannes Schefferus), 1621–1679.
> "Kununga ok Höfdinga Styrilse, hoc est, Regum Principumque Institutio. Ab Incerto Auctore Gentis Sueticae ante Saecula Nonnulla Patrio Sermone Conscripta. . . . " In *Sermonem Latinum Vertit, Notisque Necessariis Illustravit Joannes Schefferus.* Holmiae Suecorum, 1669. 234 p.

> BM CtY MH NcD

1563   *The Scheme of Universal Brotherhood; or the Christian System of Mutual Assistance . . . Insuring the Happiness and Innocence of All Mankind.* London, 1842(?). 134 p.

> BM CSmH CtY MH NN

1564   Schinagel, Géza, M.D., 1893–.
> *Possibilities.* Boston, 1930. 125 p.

> DLC

1565   [Scotti, Giulio Clemente] (*pseud.* Lucius Cornelius Europaeus), 1602–1669.
> *Lucii Cornelii Europaei Monarchia Solipsorum ad Leonem Allatium.* Venice, 1645. 144 p.

> BN ICN   1648: Bod CSmH MH   1651: DLC
> 1721: BM

1566   [——————].
> *La Monarchie des Solipses, Traduite de l'Original Latin de*

Melchior Inchofer. Translated by Pierre Restant. Amsterdam, 1721. 407 p.

BM BN   1722: ICN NN   1754: CtY ICN NcD

1567   Secrétan, Charles, 1815–1895.
Mon Utopie; Nouvelles Études Morales et Sociales. Paris, 1892. 303 p.

BM BN CtY DLC MH

1568   Sensney, Walter H. (*pseud.*). *See* Horner, Jacob W.

1569   Shaw, George Bernard, 1856–1950.
Back to Methuselah. A Metabiological Pentateuch. London, 1920. 267 p.

1921: BM BN CtY DLC ICN ICU NcD NN

1570   Sherburne, Henry.
The Oriental Philanthropist, or, True Republican. Portsmouth, N.H., 1800. 215 p.

BM CSmH CtY DLC ICN ICU MH NN

1571   Sidney, Sir Philip, 1554–1586.
The Countesse of Pembrokes Arcadia. London, 1590. 360 p.

BM CSmH CtY ICN   1593: MH   1598: NcD
1599: ICU NN   1605: BN   1891: DLC

1572   Smith, David Eugene (*pseud.* David Dunham), 1860–1944.
Every Man a Millionaire; a Baloon Trip in the Mathematical Stratosphere of Social Relations. New York, 1937. 97 p.
DLC NcD NN

1573   [Sobius, Jacobus], *d.* 1527(?).
Philalethis, Civis Utopiensis Dialensis Dialogus, de Facultatibus Rhomanensium Nuper Publicatis, Henno Rusticus. Basle, 1520.

BN Bod CtY ICN

1574   Stubbe, Henry (Stubbs, Stubbes, Stubs), 1632–1676.
The Commonwealth of Oceana Put into the Ballance, and Found Too Light. London, 1606. 15 p.

BM MH

1575 —————.

    Campanella Revived. London, 1670. 22 p.

    BM CSmH CtY DLC MH

1576 Stubbes, Phillip (Stubbs), *fl.* 1581–1593.

    The Anatomie of Abuses: Containing a Discoverie, or Briefe Summarie of Such Notable Vices and Imperfections, as Now Raigne in Many Christian Countreyes of the Worlde: but (Especiallie) in a Verie Famous Ilande Called Ailgna . . . Made Dialogue-Wise by Phillip Stubbes. London, 1583. 232 p.

    BM CSmH ICN MH   1585: CtY   1836: NN
    1870: NcD   1877: BN

1577 Suárez de Figueroa, Christóbal (Figueroa, Christóbal Suárez de), 1571–1645.

    La Constante Amarilis. Prosas y Versos. Valencia, 1609. 282 p.

    BM CtY   1614: ICN NcD   1781: BN DLC ICU MH

1578 Swan, Herbert E.

    It Might Be. A Story of the Future Progress of the Sciences, the Wonderful Advancement in the Methods of Government and the Happy State of the People. Stafford, Kan., 1896. 180 p.

    DLC MH NcD

1579 Swanwick, Anna, 1813–1899.

    An Utopian Dream and How It May be Realized. London, 1888. 55 p.

    BM

1580 Taber, Albert Ernest.

    Work for All. A Cooperative Commonwealth Based on Ruskin's Teaching. Leeds, 1914. 100 p.

    BM

1581 *Tesoro Politico in Cui Si Contengono Relationi, Instruttioni, Trattati, & Varii Discorsi, Pertinenti Alla Perfetta Intelligenza della*

Ragion di Stato. 3 vols. Milan, 1600. (Dedicatory epistle signed "Giorgio Greco.")

BM ICN NcD

1582   Thimbleby, John.
Monadelphia; or, the Formation of a New System of Society. Barnet, Eng., 1832. 76 p.

BM CtY NN

1583   Tigurinus, Chelidonius. *See* Boaistuau de Launay, Pierre.

1584   Torres, Juan de, 1547–1599.
Philosophia Moral de Principes, para su Buena Crianca y Govierno. Burgos, 1596. 953 p.

BM NcD

1585   [Townsend, Frederic.]
Ghostly Colloquies. New York, 1856. 267 p.

BM CSmH DLC ICU MH NcD NN

1586   Tracy, Roger Sherman (*pseud.* T. Shirby Hodge), 1841–1926.
The White Man's Burden; a Satirical Forecast. Boston, 1915. 225 p.

CtY DLC MH NcD NN

1587   *The Travels of Zoroaster, King of the Bactrians. Composed Chiefly for the Instruction of a Young Prince.* 3 vols. London, 1753.

CtY DLC MH

1588   *The Treasurie of Ancient and Modern Times . . . Translated out of that Worthy Spanish Gentleman, Pedro Mexio. And M. Francesco Sansovino.* Translated by Thomas Milles. 2 vols. London, 1613.

BM DLC ICN ICU NcD NN

1589   Trowbridge, Oliver R.
BiSocialism, the Reign of the Man at the Margin. New York, 1903. 427 p.

DLC ICN ICU MH NN

1590   Vida, Marco Girolamo, bishop of Alba (Marcus Hieronymus Vida Cremonensis), 1485–1566.
Dialogi de Reipublicae Dignitate. Cremona, 1556. 110 p.
BM CtY DLC ICN   1567: NN

1591   Viganò, Francesco, 1807–1891.
Battello Sotto Marino. Romanzo Bizzarro. Milan, 1839. 178 p.
NcD

1592   *Voyage de Guibray, ou les Aventures de Princes de B. et de C.* N.p., 1704.
BN

1593   [Wallace, Robert], 1697–1771.
Various Prospects of Mankind, Nature, and Providence. London, 1761. 406 p.
BM CtY DLC ICN ICU MH NcD

1594   Walsh, Walter, 1857–1931.
The World Rebuilt. London, 1917. 95 p.
BM Bod ICN MH NN

1595   Warner, Frank E. (*pseud.*). *See* Frankenstein, Ernst.

1596   [Wellman, Bert J.]
The Legal Revolution of 1902. By a Law-Abiding Revolutionist. Chicago, 1898. 334 p.
DLC MH NN

1597   Wells, Herbert George, 1866–1946.
[Almost all the works of Wells not listed as utopian could be included here as related to utopian literature.]

1598   Werdenhagen, Johannes Angelius von, 1581–1652.
Universalis Introductio in Omnes Respublicas, Sive Politica Generalis. Amsterdam, 1632. 767 p.
BM CSmH CtY DLC ICN ICU NN

1599   Weyhe, Eberhard von (Durus de Pasculo or Pascolo), 1553–1629.
       Aulicus Politicus Diversis Regulis . . . Instructus. Leipzig,
       1590(?).
       1596: BM CtY   1597: NN   1599: CSmH   1615: ICN

1600   Whitman, John Pratt.
       Utopia Dawns. Boston, 1934. 145 p.
       DLC MH NcD NN

1601   [Wilkins, John], 1614–1672.
       The Discovery of a World in the Moone, Or, a Discourse Tending to Prove That 'Tis Probable There May Be Another Habitable World in That Planet. London, 1638. 209 p.
       BM CSmH CtY DLC ICN ICU MH NN   1684: BN

1602   [————].
       A Discourse Concerning a New World & Another Planet. In Two Books. The First Book . . . A Discourse Concerning a New Planet. Tending to Prove, That 'Tis Probable Our Earth Is One of the Planets. The Second Book, Now First Published. 2 vols. in 1. London, 1640. 488 p.
       BM BN CSmH CtY DLC ICN ICU MH NcD
       1684: NN

1603   Winstanley, Gerrard, 1609–1660(?).
       The Law of Freedom in a Platform: or, True Magistracy Restored. London, 1652. 98 p.
       BM CSmH ICU

1604   ————.
       "The Law of Freedom. . . . " In *The Works of Gerrard Winstanley,* edited by George H. Sabine, pp. 501–600. Ithaca, N.Y., 1941.
       BM CSmH CtY DLC ICN ICU MH NcD NN

1605   Yelverton, Christopher.
       Oneiros; or, Some Questions of the Day. London, 1889. 246 p.
       BM DLC ICU NN

1606   Young, Michael Dunlop, 1915–.
        The Rise of the Meritocracy: 1870–2033. London, 1958. 160 p.

        BM Bod CtY DLC ICU MH NcD NN

1607   [Zacharie de Lisieux] (Louis Fontaines, Petrus Firmianus), 1582–1661.
        Gyges Gallus, Somnia Sapientis et Genius Saeculi. Paris, 1659.

        ICN NN   1671: BM Bod   1686: DLC

1608   Zahn, Oswald Francis, 1874–.
        Let's Triumvirate; or, Man, Government, and Happiness, a Philosophy of Man and a World-Wide Government Founded upon Laws of Nature. San Diego, Calif., 1943. 381 p.

        CtY DLC ICU

Short-title Index

All titles of original works are included, those of the utopian bibliography (entries 1–1232) and of the supplementary listing (entries 1233–1608).

Short-title Index

The Angel of the Revolution, 468
An Anglo-American Alliance, 1319
Animal Farm, 114
Annals of the Twenty-Ninth Century, 113
L'Anno 3000, 748
Anno Domini 2000, 1143
Anno Domini 2071, 528
Anno 2065, 527
Annus Sophiae Jubilaeus, 1237
El Año Mil Novecientos, 974
Another World, 331
Another World . . . Montalluyah, 711
Antangil, 718, 719
Antéaur, 34
Anticipation, 936
"Anti-Fanatical Religion," 1402
L'Anti Hermaphrodite, 912
Antiquity Reviv'd, 36
Antorcha Universal del Porvenir, 297
Ape and Essence, 603
Apollon Mentor, 879
L'Arcadie, 1549
Ardinghello, 1428
Areostiade, 654
Argenis, 1253
Aristocracy, 848
Aristokia, 917
Aristopia, 578
Armata, 322, 323
"The Arrival in London of Vela," 815
Artemidoro, 1091
L'Arti Liberali et Mecaniche, 129
"As Easy as ABC," 641
"Asem," 441
"The Assassins," 1027
Asses in Clover, 858
Astolfo, 738
The Astonishing Island, 579
Astreada, 48
At the End of the World, 479

Athonia, 1014
Atlanta, 969
Atlantis, 1356
Au Pays de l'Harmonie, 271
"Au Pays de Liberté," 763
Auf zum Weltreich, 1035
Aulicus Politicus, 1599
The Aurora Phone, 220
L'Aurore de la Civilisation, 1054
Les Avantures de Télémaque, 341
L'Avenir, 1449
L'Avenir . . . Nouveau Contrat Social, 1270
Les Aventures d'Abdalla, 1284
Les Aventures de Nono, 455
Aventures Extraordinaires d'un Savant Russe, 673

Back to Methuselah, 1569
Back to the Soil, 1401
Balmanno, 893
Barclay His Argenis, 1252
Baron Grimbosh, 729
The Basiliade, 811
Battello Sotto Marino, 1591
Beatrice the Sixteenth, 214
Die Befreiung, 50
The Beginning, 75
Bensalem and New Jerusalem, 997
Bentivolio and Urania, 1437
Beschryvinge van . . . Krinke Kesmes, 1044
The Best Is Yet to Be, 1502
Beulah, 263
Das bey Zwey Hundert Jahr Lang Unbekannte, 58
Beyond the Black Ocean, 728
Beyond the Selvas, 399
La Biblia del Pernalismo, 903
Bilder aus der Zukunft, 661

Short-title Index

Short-title Index

Short-title Index

Short-title Index

Short-title Index

Short-title Index

Short-title Index

The New Columbia; or, The Re-United States, 920
The New Cyneas, 1346
A New Day Dawns, 116
A New Discoverie of . . . Port-Dul, 842
A New Discovery of Terra Incognita Australis, 361
New Era, 186
The New-Found Politicke, 123
The New Gulliver, 875
The New Industrial Dawn, 1327
The New Koran, 1140
The New Moon, 864
The New Regime, 141
The New Republic, 742, 743
The New Republic: Founded on the . . . Rights of Man, 1005
The New Utopia, 302
The New Utopia, or England in 1985, 1114
A New Voyage to the East-Indies, 793
A New Voyage to the Island of Fools, 1163
The New Voyage to Utopia, 333
New Voyages to North America, 1448
Newaera, 555
News from Nowhere, 823
Newtopia, 1202
The Next Generation, 740
The Next Ninety-three, 1167
Nicodème dans la Lune, 73
Nicolai Klimii, 575
Nieuwe Reis Naar Utopia, 1138
The Night Land, 574
Nineteen Eighty-Four, 115
1944, 510
Nineteen Hundred?, 546
Nineteen Hundred and Seventy-Five, 849
1931: . . . the Twentieth Century, 533
The Nineteenth Century, 314

'96; a Romance of Utopia, 983
No Borderland, 820
Lo Noche Encantada, 613
Noland, 395
Le Nouveau Cynée, 1345
Le Nouveau Gulliver, 275
Nouveau Mémoire . . . des Cacouacs, 809
La Nouveau Panurge, 1504
Le Nouveau Télémaque, 653
Nouveaux Voyages de . . . Lahontan, 1447
La Nouvelle Atlantide, 944
Nouvelle Relation . . . dans l'Îsle de Naudely, 683
Nova Solyma the Ideal City, 449
Novae Solymae, 448

O-Brazile, 1426
Observations upon Experimental Philosophy, 844
Oceana, 519
Of Councils and Counselors, 1395
Olbie, 1002
Olombia, 1151
One Hundred Years Hence, 316
One of "Berrian's" Novels, 1071
One Wise Rich Man, 1171
Oneiros, 1605
The Open Conspiracy, 1182
L'Optique, 1414
Opusculum Eruditum, 1278
L'Orient Vierge, 757
The Oriental Philanthropist, 1570
The Original . . . Account of . . . Acaniba, 1546
L'Orologe des Princes, 483
Orphan Island, 723
The Other Side of the Sun, 183
Our Coming World, 786

215

Short-title Index

Short-title Index

Short-title Index

Short-title Index

Short-title Index

Chronological Index

The dates are those of the earliest writing and/or publication insofar as it is known. All original works are included, those of the utopian bibliography (entries 1–1232) and of the supplementary listing (entries 1233–1608).

Chronological Index

Chronological Index

Chronological Index

227

Chronological Index